# THE BIBLE

# ON THE BORDER

# THE BIBLE

# ON THE BORDER

*How Father Rick Thomas and his friends
learned to serve the poor of Mexico
by taking God at His word.*

## RICHARD DUNSTAN

✝

THE LORD'S RANCH PRESS
VADO, NEW MEXICO

*Imprimatur:*
*Most Reverend Ricardo Ramirez*
*Bishop of Las Cruces,*
*Las Cruces, New Mexico*
*January 2, 2009*

Published by The Lord's Ranch Press, Vado, New Mexico

Printed and bound in the United States of America.

Cover design by: Jorge Baeza

ISBN #: 978-0-9821170-1-9

### Photo Credits

**Photo on back cover** – © Matthew Dunstan
**Photos** 2, 7, 12, 16, 17, 19, 21, 25, 27 – © Richard Dunstan
**Photo** 18 – courtesy of the Nevarez family
**Photo** 33 – courtesy of the Halloran family
**Photos** front cover, 1, 3-6, 8-11, 13-15, 20, 21-24, 26, 28-32, 34-37 – courtesy of Our Lady's Youth Center archives.

*To Mary—my wife,*
*my best friend, my spiritual rock.*

# CONTENTS

Foreword by Ralph Martin ............................................................9

Introduction..............................................................................11

Prelude.....................................................................................13

**Part I:** OLYC Ministries, Past and Present ......................21

  Chapter 1: By the Banks of the Rio Grande............................21

  Chapter 2: How it All Began ...................................................31

  Chapter 3: The Ministries Today..............................................41

      Las Alas ...................................................................44

      The Lord's Ranch .....................................................45

      Food Bank and Clinic in Juarez................................47

      Jail and Mental Hospital Ministries .........................49

      The Dump Ministry .................................................49

      Miscellaneous ........................................................50

  Chapter 4: The People of OLYC ..............................................53

  Chapter 5: Mighty Works of God .............................................93

**Part II:** Spiritual Principles ...............................................103

  Chapter 6: Discerning God's Will............................................103

  Chapter 7: Working in God's Power.........................................113

  Chapter 8: Always the Poor ...................................................123

  Chapter 9: Go and Make Disciples .........................................133

  Chapter 10: A Tale of Two Kingdoms......................................141

      Cleansing Prayer ....................................................152

Chapter 11: The One Thing Lacking................................... 153

**Part III:** Putting it Together............................................ 163

Chapter 12: Trying This at Home................................ 163

What to Do........................................................... 164

What to Watch Out For....................................... 166

Epilogue.................................................................... 171

Afterword: The Kingdom of God has Come Near................... 177

# FOREWORD

BY RALPH MARTIN
President of Renewal Ministries

Every now and then extraordinary men and women appear who show us new possibilities of knowing who God is and what is possible when we surrender to Him. Father Rick Thomas was one of those men. People gathered around him, ministering to the poor in the dumps of Juarez, El Paso, and elsewhere, and now, even after his death, they continue to carry on the mission.

And what is that mission? It's about serving the poor, of course, but it's actually far more radical than that. It's about reverencing and obeying the Word of God and the inspirations of the Spirit in unreserved generosity and overflowing, non-sentimental love.

Often our first response to special men and women like this is to take a moment to admire them, and then go on with our lives. Business as usual. But Father Rick Thomas doesn't make it easy for us to do that. He insists that living the Gospel isn't just an option for those especially called. Rather, it is a call for total surrender – a call addressed to every Christian.

Richard Dunstan, that rare combination of a professional writer who also has a profound grasp of the subject he is writing about, helps us to get the message of Father Rick Thomas and apply it to our own lives and circumstances. Like the man he's writing about, Richard doesn't leave us the option of putting Father Rick on a pedestal and avoiding the challenge his life and work presents to all of us.

It's rare to find people like Father Rick Thomas who live the Gospel with such zeal and believe it with such conviction. It is also rare to find a writer such as Richard Dunstan who is able both to understand and communicate how this applies to all of us.

Father Rick and Richard have found each other, and we are all the richer.

# INTRODUCTION

When Father Rick Thomas suggested to Richard Dunstan that he write a book about the ministries of Our Lady's Youth Center, Richard agreed and took on the project whole-heartedly. Little did Richard know how long the endeavor would take. It has spanned two decades and involved many trips down from his home in Canada, countless hours interviewing people, and much writing, editing and updating.

Father Rick placed a lot of confidence in Richard and made it a priority in his very busy schedule to be available for interviews that would often last for several hours at a time. In fact, in the 20-plus years that I served as Father Rick's secretary I never saw him dedicate so much time to a writing project as he did to this one. Even when he was weak and in pain during his final days, Father Rick rallied his strength to meet with Richard for what would turn out to be the last interviews of his life. As a result Richard has captured firsthand from this remarkable and holy priest some of the extraordinary marvels God has done in our midst.

Father Thomas did not live to see this book published, but I know for certain that he would have been very pleased with how it turned out. We who are continuing the work and legacy that Father Thomas left behind make it our sincere prayer that this book will both challenge and bless you.

*Ellen Hogarty*
*President of the Board of Directors*
*Our Lady's Youth Center*

# PRELUDE

*The death of a priest, the life of the Bible*

The homemade plywood coffin was all Father Rick Thomas, S.J., took for himself. The two bishops, the seventeen priests, and the elbow-to-elbow crowd—rich and poor, young and old, Hispanic and Anglo—were testimony to what he left behind for others.

A thousand people crammed the funeral Mass at El Paso's Sacred Heart Church May 12, 2006, to say goodbye to the priest they loved. And they all roared to their feet in applause when Bishop Ricardo Ramirez of neighboring Las Cruces, NM, reminded them of why they loved him.

"If there is anyone I have ever known who in our lives exemplifies the life of the Church as expressed in the Acts of the Apostles, it was Father Rick Thomas," said the longtime friend Father Thomas called "Tocayo" (namesake).

Then the bishop waited patiently until the clapping had died down and the people had taken their seats. "I

13

believe the applause that he wants is the applause to be lived in our lives," he told the crowd: "that we continue his work, those of us who are left here."

"His work"— and the work of about 150 other people in the adjoining border cities of El Paso and Ciudad Juarez, Mexico—was just what Bishop Ramirez said: bringing to 21st-century life, not only the Book of Acts, but the entire Bible. The book in your hands, conceived and mostly written with Father Thomas's co-operation, is about how he and his friends did exactly that; and with his death, sixteen days after our last interview, it is my hope that it will help make sure we "continue his work," not only in El Paso and Juarez (his friends and his Friend will see to that), but in other towns and cities, across North America and beyond.

The key to this work is the fact that Father Thomas and his friends have discovered that the Bible is true *now*. Most of the time, when folks argue about whether the Bible is true, they mean *then*—for example, did Jesus literally multiply five loaves of bread and two fishes to make enough food for a crowd of more than five thousand? But Father Thomas's friends are way past that. They have discovered that Jesus multiplies food *today*, and yes, literally: most famously burritos and ham and baloney sandwiches on Christmas Day in 1972 (see Chapter 1), but also many times since then. Or some may argue about whether Jonah's stay in the stomach of a large fish is a historical fact; but the people around Father Thomas are too busy to get involved in that argument. They're busy looking for ways to obey God's command to Jonah: "Get up, go to Nineveh, that great city, and proclaim to it the message that I tell you." (Jonah 3:2)

14

They preach the Gospel inside Mexican jails—sometimes even locked in with the prisoners, with no guards present. They hold retreats for people from all over the world on a ranch in the desert. They give away food every week to two hundred families in the shantytowns of Juarez. They hold weekly prayer meetings in downtown El Paso. They operate a dirt-cheap medical clinic (free for those who can't afford cheap). They broadcast Bible readings worldwide by shortwave radio. They pray over the physically and mentally ill, and a lot of those people recover.

But those are just details; they've changed before and they'll change again—some of them, maybe, before this book is printed. Here are the constants: these people *trust* what the Bible tells them, they *do* what the Bible tells them, and they expect to see *God do today* what the Bible tells them He did two thousand years ago. And guess what? He does.

What's more, God pays the bills. The community doesn't fundraise in any systematic way, and the more dedicated members work full-time at the ministries, without pay. "You received without payment," says the Bible (Matt. 10:8b); "give without payment."

I first met Father Thomas and his friends in 1989, after reading about them in a magazine article. I have been back to visit half a dozen times since then. I've been most of the places they go, including the locked jail cells (now *there* was an initiation) and the scrap lumber and adobe and concrete block houses of west Juarez. I've seen what their work does for the poor, and I've also seen what it does for the community itself. I'm a worldly

15

man and I've been to lots of parties, but I've never seen anybody having more fun than this crowd.

I have, in short, seen the Gospel in action, bumping along the streets of Juarez on the way to the jail or the food bank, and I know what's happening is real. I'm writing this book because I believe that this is a story every Christian needs to hear. Because this way of life doesn't have to be limited to El Paso and Juarez. You and I can live it, too, in our own home towns. There's even a list of guidelines for doing that, near the end of the book. And while I can't claim that I really *have* tried it at home yet, I haven't given up on the idea either. Maybe we can do it together.

\*\*\*\*\*

A few things need to be explained before the story begins. First of all, the community this book is about grew out of an El Paso ministry called Our Lady's Youth Center, OLYC for short, and still operates under that legal name. But today the work has expanded far beyond youth activities, and has diversified and decentralized to the point that no one person knows everything that's going on. Even the figure cited above, 150 people involved in the ministries, is really just an educated guess. Most decisions are made at the lowest level of organization, and nobody, not even Father Thomas, has ever been in charge in the strictest administrative sense. To keep things simple, I will be writing about "the OLYC community" or "OLYC volunteers" throughout the book, but the reader should understand that the reality is more complicated than that.

Secondly, as its name suggests, Our Lady's Youth Center is a Roman Catholic organization, obedient in every way—let me stress that point—to the Catholic Church. I'm a Catholic myself, and there will be a lot of Catholic references in this book. But the basic spiritual principles followed by the OLYC community are not restricted to Catholics. Non-Catholic Christians are welcome in the OLYC ministries, and some have made huge contributions to the work. Protestant or Orthodox Christians who want to do similar work in their own communities can do so within their own denominations.

Third, OLYC is charismatic, complete with speaking in tongues and the other charismatic gifts. But the work isn't restricted to charismatics either, at least not in the stereotypical sense. The point of OLYC's ministries is not tongues but the power of God, and you don't have to speak in tongues to participate in that power.

Fourth, this book is not mainly about miracles. Most of the publicity the OLYC community has gotten over the years has been concerned with reports of miracles – especially Father Rene Laurentin's 1982 book *Miracles in El Paso?* The cold, hard fact is that the answer to the question in Father Laurentin's title is "we don't know," because OLYC does not bother documenting miracles to satisfy Vatican commissions or any other body. This book contains a good many reports of apparent miracles (or as the New Testament actually calls them, "deeds of power" or "signs") from those who witnessed them; but while I certainly believe that these things really happened and that they are God's work in one way or another, I don't claim to know how many of them are technically miraculous.

17

Finally, it is neither a biography of Father Thomas nor a complete history of the community. Many things worth knowing about Father Thomas, and many people who played important roles over the years, have been left for another time.

Instead, this book is aimed at investigating and explaining the spiritual principles that operate in OLYC's ministries: how God's power works there, how the people co-operate with it, and how the rest of us can do the same. Some of it, for sure, is pretty spectacular, but as Father Thomas said, "a lot of it's really ordinary. Unload the truck. Put gas in the truck. Check the tires for air." In a sentence, this book is about how to put God's gas in your truck and drive it where He wants it to go.

The book is divided into three parts. Part I could be called description. There's an overview chapter: the story of the 1972 Christmas dinner multiplication, a look at El Paso and Juarez, a day in the life of OLYC's ministries. Next come a chapter on the history of the community, a list and description of current and past ministries, a look at a few of the people who make up the community, and a collection of "deeds of power" as reported by community members.

Part II is explanations. There are chapters on the key concept of obedience to God; on work with the poor; on evangelism; on the power of God; on spiritual warfare; and on the "one thing lacking" that keeps even a group like OLYC from the full triumph of God's kingdom.

Part III is the shortest, but if this book is going to have any value in eternity, it will be the most important. It's an explanation of how the rest of us can do at home, in our own towns and cities, what OLYC has done in El Paso and Juarez. There's also an epilogue on Father Thomas's last days, and there's a personal afterword on some points that happen to be especially important to me as an individual.

The vast majority of the information in this book comes from interviews with members of the OLYC community, especially Father Thomas, together with personal observations of their work. Father Thomas checked an earlier draft of the manuscript for accuracy, and other leaders have done the same for the final version, but they have not dictated its organization or interfered with my own comments.

Within minutes of arriving at OLYC for my first visit, I spotted a dog-eared piece of paper thumbtacked to a bulletin board, carrying a motto that has summed up OLYC's work for me ever since: "For the kingdom of God depends not on talk but on power." (1 Cor 4:20) I have talked enough now; let's observe God's power in action, in this steadfast outpost of His kingdom.

# PART I: OLYC MINISTRIES, PAST AND PRESENT

## CHAPTER 1: BY THE BANKS OF THE RIO GRANDE

The story may be hard to believe, but it's easy enough to tell. On Christmas Day, 1972, a couple of dozen prayer group members from El Paso, Texas, drove a few blocks down the street and across the Rio Grande into Mexico. Across the river, a few friends from the border city, Ciudad Juarez, joined them. They were all headed for the Juarez municipal dump, with a load of ham, burritos and baloney sandwiches, all intended as a surprise Christmas dinner for the ragpickers who lived in cardboard shacks surrounding the smoldering heaps of garbage.

The prayer group people, from a Catholic ministry called Our Lady's Youth Center, were just trying to obey God. They'd been studying the Bible, three hours a day, and as Christmas came along they ran across Luke 14:13, which says to invite the poor to your banquets instead of your relatives or friends.

"That passage really touched us," recalls Frank Alarcon, who was an El Paso postman at the time.

"None of us had ever complied with that. We decided we were going to share our dinner with the poorest people we knew, the people at the dump."

So they got together the food—tamales, burritos, a big ham, candy for the children. Alarcon brought twenty-five baloney sandwiches, his favorite meal. "We made enough for 150 people," he says. "We thought that was a lot."

Christmas morning came, cold, cloudy and damp. Several carloads of volunteers headed out to the dump, which was well outside the built-up part of Juarez at the time. There they found the ragpickers on the job, Christmas or no Christmas. Unfortunately, they were divided into two unions that didn't get along at all. That was a surprise, but the OLYC people prayed and negotiated a settlement: the two unions would eat together on neutral ground—the part of the dump where both groups sold their trash to a government contractor.

Then came a bigger problem. As the volunteers set up tables made from plywood and oil drums, more and more people got wind of the free food and started rolling in over the hills of garbage, more than 300 people in all—double the number the group had prepared for. Father Rick Thomas, the Jesuit priest in charge of OLYC, stood up, apologized for the shortage of food, and promised to share it for as long as it lasted.

He needn't have apologized. The food did not run out, no matter how many people came.

Alarcon remembers standing on top of his pickup camper to watch the scene. He saw children line up, take their share of the candy, then get back in line; nobody could stop them. He saw volunteers handing out an endless stream of burritos. He saw the ham being sliced, and sliced, and sliced: "I'm talking about big slices."

"Everybody's eating and having a good time," he recalls. "Nobody's arguing. Everybody got everything they wanted. Some of them got little bags of food to take home. We still had enough food to give to two orphanages on the way home.

"We all went home that evening floating on Cloud 9. Then it started to dawn on us what had happened. That day we met Jesus face to face."

The story of the multiplication of the Christmas dinner has been told many times. In fact, this time might be once too often. Father Thomas got tired of reading about how the miracle of 1972 was the foundational event for all OLYC's ministries. The real foundational event, he said, was the group's decision to take God at His word, and Luke 14:13 is just one example of that.

Today OLYC runs food banks, a medical clinic, a jail evangelism program, a ranch, an inner healing ministry, and a Scripture-only radio station. That isn't an exhaustive list. The whole operation is so far out on the limb of faith that you'd think the whole tree would tip over. The group doesn't even fundraise, because the Bible says God will provide, and some community members have quit good-paying jobs to work full-time without pay, because the Bible says to "give without payment." But the limb of faith never seems to break, and Father Thomas and his friends long ago stopped worrying about it. After all, the Bible also says not to worry.

"We have discovered that God is real, His Word is real, and it's to be taken seriously," Father Thomas said.

"He'll take it as seriously as you do."

\*\*\*\*\*\*\*\*\*\*\*\*

There's nothing grand about the Rio Grande where OLYC workers cross it. It's more of a moat than a river, a narrow stream trapped in a concrete channel with a heavy barbed-wire-and-chain-link fence along the American side, just one more piece of Border Patrol equipment along with the green-and-white squad cars that park along the riverbank to watch for illegal immigrants. But as it trickles between Juarez (population estimated as high as two million) on the south and El Paso (700,000 not counting illegals) on the north, the Rio Grande marks the biggest collision of rich and poor populations on the face of the earth.

"We have the poor so close to us," says Ellen Hogarty, a fortysomething OLYC worker who joined the community at age 18 and is now president of the board of directors. "We can go across the border and instantly be in the homes of people who live in Third World conditions.

"It changes you. How can we minister to our brothers and sisters and not be changed, not repent?"

El Paso-based OLYC volunteers do cross that border nearly every day, bouncing along in vans on their way to meet other volunteers who live in Juarez. Together they ride off to the day's ministry, praying all the way: the rosary, Scripture passages such as Psalm 68 or 103, and a ferocious four-page prayer against Satan dating back more than 100 years to Pope Leo XIII. The devil has been at work in some of the places they're going, and they're ready for a battle.

Let's say it's Wednesday. That's the day for the Juarez municipal jails and mental hospital. In charge is Anita Osuna of Juarez. The workers, perhaps two dozen strong, assemble in the lobby of the first jail and read the prayer against Satan aloud, one group in English and the other in Spanish. Then in they file, past waiting jail visitors, dropping off driver's licenses or other ID with jail guards to be picked up on the way out.

Once inside, the women gather in a safe spot and pray while the men divide up and visit the cells. "Visiting," when jail officials permit, means being locked in, half a dozen volunteers with no guards present and as many as 40 prisoners sprawled on the benches or the floor. There's no other furniture except a toilet in the corner. Most of the inmates are in jail—this time—for minor offences like public drunkenness or fighting, but many of them have done worse things than that, and some have even killed.

Inside the cells, or just outside if necessary, the men preach the Gospel, like Catholic Billy Grahams. Their "altar call" is an invitation to kneel and pray, and maybe half the prisoners do that. Afterwards, all the inmates get sandwiches and lemonade, plus Catholic sacramentals: holy water and blessed salt.

Then it's off to the mental hospital. It's still pretty rough to a visiting gringo, but compared to the jail it's not so bad. Many of the inmates are free to roam the courtyard, and even watch TV in the recreation room. The visitors sing and hand out refreshments, and some go from room to room praying with the people they find.

I can't help remembering an earlier visit to the hospital with Father Thomas. One inmate, a man in his 20s named Jose, wasn't interested, but Father Thomas didn't give up easily. "You want to get out of here?" he asked in Spanish. "God has power." Eventually Jose agreed, and the group prayed for his needs, then led him in asking Jesus to come into his life. Inmates the group prays for often do "get out of here" a lot faster than anyone was expecting, Father Thomas said.

Both the jail and the mental hospital have changed a fair bit since the volunteers began visiting in 1979. The mental hospital was even seedier than it is now, with most of the patients locked in their rooms. And as for the jail—well, the only reason the OLYC volunteers got access to the jail was that the administrator had invited them because he thought God was the only hope for the hard-core prisoners.

The prisoners didn't agree, and neither did the guards. On the first visit about 30 OLYC people went into the courtyard with a bullhorn, but the prisoners and guards drowned them out, shouting insults and mockery. So the volunteers just sang, prayed and read Scripture. For an hour and a half. Especially Phil. 2:10-11: "...at the name of Jesus every knee should bend..."

"And it happened," recalls Mary Ann Halloran, who was there on that first visit even though she was in the final month of pregnancy. "They got quiet, and they wanted the prayer."

"There was total silence in the jail," Father Thomas said. "The ones we could see were on their knees. The administrator let them out in the courtyard, and every one of them received prayer."

The prisoners aren't always friendly even today, but they're quiet and co-operative. Some of them get healings, some of them turn up at prayer meetings or other OLYC ministries after they get out. But the group doesn't have the resources for a follow-up program, so there's really no way to measure the lasting effects.

"It's a seed-planting," Father Thomas said.

After leaving the mental hospital, the vans visit a second jail in another part of the city, then bounce back over the bridge to El Paso and OLYC's headquarters at Las Alas (pronounced lahs AH-lahs, Spanish for "the wings"), where downtown office buildings begin to mix with the grimy border district. Las Alas workers head off to a late lunch at a restaurant owned by Tommy and Ceci Barrientos, OLYC community members whose way to "give without payment" is feeding the gang from Las Alas without charge after the noon rush hour.

Wednesday is prayer meeting night at Las Alas, and a crowd anywhere from one hundred to three hundred fills the chairs for three hours of music, prayer, and

27

Mass. The evening begins with most of the crowd snaking through the chairs in a conga line to high-volume praise songs, mostly in Spanish. Then children and teenagers—there are plenty of both—head off to their own teaching sessions, while the adults stay behind for theirs. A volunteer provides translation into Spanish or English, as needed.

There's no collection, except a basket at the door for donations to the Juarez dump ministry. After Mass, volunteers hand out tapes of Father Thomas's teachings, mostly for free.

Las Alas itself is something close to a miracle, although it would never qualify in front of any Vatican commission. After many years in a dumpy old building deeper in the border slum, OLYC was looking for new headquarters in 1996 when a 100-by-200-foot department store on a full city block lot came on the market during a business reorganization. Racing a deadline set by the bank, three deep-pocketed agencies including the State of Texas bid on the property. OLYC also put in an offer for what Father Thomas called a "pitiful" amount, definitely the low bid.

Then surprising things started happening. One of the major bidders dropped out when it found a better deal somewhere else. The second was disqualified because a government official enforced a technicality that's normally ignored. The biggest shock, though, was what happened to the State of Texas bid. "They're the eight-hundred-pound gorilla," says Mike Ridley, the realtor who handled the sale. "Whatever they want, they get." However, the official state offer included a condition the bank couldn't accept: the building had to be demolished by the vendor before the sale. This condition could not be removed in time to meet the deadline. Only the OLYC offer was left standing.

"To this day nobody from the state can find out how that mistake was made," says Ridley. Ridley, a Presbyterian, lost a lot of commission on the deal, but he says he saw the hand of God in it at an early stage and decided just to enjoy the experience. "God already had a plan—He wanted the father [Thomas] to have that building," Ridley says. "It's one of the most inspiring things that ever happened to me."

For Father Thomas, though, getting Las Alas, with no frills but plenty of room for all OLYC's activities, was just one more example of a process he had gotten used to over the years.

"We're well aware of God's providence working all the time in a marvelous way," he said. "But it's not miraculous. The Lord has a rhythm and a timing, and if you're in His timing it works out great.

"The whole aim is to do God's will. He co-operates in what you're doing as you co-operate in what He's doing."

## CHAPTER 2: HOW IT ALL BEGAN

To do God's will. That's what every Christian is supposed to want, and Rick Thomas had been working at it for years. But he was past 40 before he found out how to go about it effectively.

Born in Florida in 1928, Father Thomas was ordained in 1958 and began his priesthood teaching high school in New Orleans. In 1964 he was sent to El Paso, to take over OLYC.

The high school was an elite institution. The youth center was a battered old building in the middle of a slum. But the two places had a lot in common. It's safe to say the people in charge, Father Thomas included, were trying to do God's will, but the work was being done on human effort and measured by human standards. And that left a gap.

"The high school was outstanding in every way except spiritually," Father Thomas recalled. "It wasn't a priority. In El Paso, I was very successful exteriorly, in that the youth center had all kinds of activities and it looked good. But I knew there wasn't any kind of significant spiritual fruit.

"It was discouraging. I was giving it the best shot I had, but I didn't see any results."

Then came the charismatic renewal.

Non-charismatics, if they think of the renewal at all nowadays, usually think first of the incomprehensible vocal sounds known to charismatics as "speaking in tongues." The next thought might be of rowdy prayer meetings with people shouting things like "praise the Lord!" and singing songs not found in traditional Catholic hymn books. But those things aren't really the point; even after Father Thomas became a charismatic, it was years before he spoke in tongues. What's central to the charismatic experience—though obviously it isn't the exclusive property of charismatics—is an appreciation of the power of the Holy Spirit, the forgotten member of the Trinity.

Every Christian knows about God the Father. He created the universe. And by definition, every Christian knows about God the Son: Jesus. He redeemed us, dying on the cross and rising gloriously from the tomb, almost two thousand years ago. God the Holy Spirit, though, usually comes across as some sort of theological abstraction, so much so that many of us are only a step up from the disciples St. Paul met in Ephesus (Acts 19:1-7): "we have not even heard that there *is* a Holy Spirit."

But to charismatics, as for most really effective Christians down the centuries, the Holy Spirit is no abstraction. Jesus promised his disciples that they would receive *power* when the Holy Spirit had come upon them, and that promise has held good for nearly

2,000 years. The Spirit is God acting in the world *now*, not so much a concept as a bulldozer. So doing God's will becomes just a matter of following the bulldozer. We may not understand or even like where it goes, but we'll certainly see the obstacles disappear.

The charismatic renewal is usually dated as beginning in 1900, in what became known as the Pentecostal churches—"Holy Rollers," skeptics used to call them. It hit more mainstream Protestant churches in the 1960s, Catholicism in 1967. One of the early leaders in the Catholic charismatic renewal was the late Father Harold Cohen S.J., a seminary classmate of Father Thomas.

In 1969, Father Thomas visited New Orleans, and Father Cohen invited him to a prayer meeting. He accepted, but was kept away by other business and arrived after the meeting was over. A few participants waited for him and prayed over him, for what charismatics often call baptism in the Holy Spirit. Among those praying for him was Sister Mary Virginia Clark, later to be a key co-worker with Father Thomas in the 70s and 80s.

The prayer itself wasn't an impressive experience; what Father Thomas remembered best in later years was the headache he had at the time, which the prayer didn't heal. That night, though, he awoke in deep prayer, much to his surprise, and prayer has come more easily to him ever since. But for the time being, that was about it. "It wasn't like being in the dark and having the stadium lights go on," he recalled later. "It was a gradual experience."

He went back to El Paso with four pamphlets on the renewal and set up a charismatic prayer meeting as an OLYC staff retreat, but attendance was disappointing. Next came a weekly prayer meeting at Loretto Academy, in what was then a middle-class Anglo neighborhood with almost all Anglo attendance. Father Thomas didn't really know what he was doing. There was no instruction on classical charismatic subjects like speaking in tongues, or even baptism in the Spirit. The pamphlets just said to read Scripture, sing songs and serve coffee afterward. "We thought the coffee was an essential part of it," he said.

Fortunately, he said, God seemed to be running the show. The group limped along with the prayer meetings, and after one of them, the Holy Spirit stepped in while Father Thomas was away for a few minutes driving two young people home. He returned to find two teenage girls praying in tongues. One of them hadn't even been at the meeting—she had just arrived to pick the other one up afterward, and when she arrived a visitor from Arizona had offered to pray over them. The outburst of tongues was the result, a total surprise to both girls. They demanded an explanation from Father Thomas— hadn't he learned about all this in seminary?—but he had no answer for them. Then, to his astonishment, the two girls started turning up at daily Mass.

"I told God, I don't know what you're doing, but that doesn't make any difference," Father Thomas said years later. "You do what you want and I'll co-operate. I still have that attitude."

In short, Father Thomas just decided to get in behind that bulldozer, instead of blocking the way. From that day forward, he and a few others at OLYC began operating in God's power, not human effort.

"Once we give God permission, God begins to do all kinds of things," he said. "We let Him do whatever He wants, and He does incredible things."

The prayer groups spread. A weekly meeting in Spanish began at OLYC. Next came meetings at the center's youth camp, Camp Juan Diego. Evy Nelson, who was about twelve at the time, remembers Sunday prayer meetings there that would begin at 1 p.m. and run into the evening, with praise, teaching, Mass, and a community meal. Soon too, meetings were being held across the border in Juarez. But the community still had one major lesson to learn about how the power of God works.

Father Thomas had heard about ministry to the poor, much like his own but a lot more effective, going on at the Episcopal Church of the Redeemer in Houston. He went to Houston to check out the program. "The outstanding thing I saw about them was that they were studying Scripture all the time. So I said, let's start studying Scripture." And back at OLYC, Bible study it was. Three hours a day, with a dozen or more people bringing in what they had read, and the group praying over the results. It was in one of those sessions that Luke 14:13 came up, and the group decided to take Christmas dinner to the Juarez dump.

The Christmas multiplication of 1972 may not have been the foundational event for the OLYC community, but it was the turning point for the first major ministry undertaken in the newly-discovered power of the Holy

Spirit. "This was the one people talked about," says Evy Nelson. "After that, it seemed like every week had its account of some manifestation of God's Spirit moving."

Frank Alarcon and others began collecting things for the dump people. First it was food and clothes. Then came money. It started with a twenty-five-cent donation, and it grew. About 1974, when the volunteers had five hundred dollars in hand, they opened a food store at the dump. The idea was to sell food at wholesale price, "and use the same money over and over," says Alarcon. But the dump residents couldn't even afford wholesale, so the volunteers cut the price in half and made up the difference out of their own pockets. Just like Mark 10:21: "go, sell what you own, and give the money to the poor."

"They were selling their TVs and jewelry to keep the store open," Alarcon recalls.

In 1975 the dump workers formed their own co-operative and took over from a middleman who had held a government monopoly on the salvage. Adobe houses, and later cement block houses, started to replace the cardboard shacks, although the OLYC people don't take credit for that; Alarcon says it's just the natural development of a Juarez shantytown, as people settle in and gather better building materials. Alarcon retired from the post office in 1986 to run the dump ministry full time. The city government moved the dump operation away in 1994, several miles to the south and out of the populated area, but the ministry still carries on serving the poor of the neighborhood, with a variety of ministries. In 2005 the dump ministry formally separated from OLYC under its own board of directors and fundraising, but the two groups still collaborate.

In 1974, OLYC had to give up Camp Juan Diego. But in December of that year Father Thomas found 160 acres for sale near Las Cruces, New Mexico, about 40 miles north of El Paso, and the group bought the property, which it named the Lord's Ranch. In addition, the group leased 320 acres of adjoining land from the Bureau of Land Management. The BLM threatened to cancel the lease in the late 1990s in a dispute over the terms of the agreement, but supporters all over North America mounted a letter-writing campaign and the BLM allowed the group to buy the land in 2000. The same year the ranch acquired a fourth 160-acre quarter-section, bringing the property to a full square mile.

At first the volunteers used the ranch to grow food for the poor of Juarez. At one time as many as forty people lived on the site, running a dairy farm, orchards and vegetable gardens. But about 1987 the group received prophecies that God was going to change things. Sure enough, crop disease hit, and the ranch suddenly ran short of volunteers. So the community gave up farming, started buying food for the Juarez food banks—cheaper than growing it, as it turned out—and converted the ranch into what amounted to a primitive and unstructured retreat center. The last cow left in 1989.

OLYC has been running food banks at various locations since the mid-1970s. In 1981 the community was given a good-size tract of land on top of a mesa (flat-topped hill) in a poor district of west Juarez; that has been the main food bank location ever since, and a weekly medical and dental clinic was set up on the same site. Mass and a prayer meeting take place each Monday.

At one time the food bank served 700 families a week, with 50 to 80 clinic visits per week. The food bank was operated according to two scriptural passages, Deut. 14:28 (setting aside food for the widow and orphan) and 2 Thess. 3:10 ("Anyone unwilling to work should not eat"). The people who received food paid for it by working. They helped prepare and hand out the food—a huge job in itself—or did local improvement work like digging ditches and building houses for the poor. Some of the women made quilts, and the elderly prayed for everybody else.

But this all came to an end in 1993, when some of the local volunteers sued and a court ruled that they had the rights of employees under Mexican law. As a result, the leaders couldn't ask anybody to work, which meant they couldn't physically operate the food distribution. So the food operation had to be cut back drastically. But many of the families kept coming for the prayer and even brought their own meager food to share with those worse off than themselves; meanwhile, food deliveries to the homebound continued, and so did the clinics. Gradually services were restored, though on a smaller scale than before.

The community was invited into the Juarez municipal jail about 1979, but at first the leaders hesitated because they were worried about lack of follow-up. Then the late Manny Basurto, a prominent community leader at the time, said he felt an overwhelming prompting from God to go ahead with the ministry anyhow. The results of the first visit (see Chapter 1) seemed to confirm the message. Since then the jail visit has been a weekly routine of prayer, singing and preaching, with an in-cell "altar call" and distribution of food, lemonade and sacramentals. For a number of years the group also visited the nearby Judicial, a federal prison for more serious offenders where outsiders (or even relatives of prisoners) are not normally allowed, but then the Judicial was relocated, too far away to visit. More recently, the municipal jail was moved from the original "stone jail," an antiquated hellhole with concrete benches and smelly toilets, across the street to the cleaner and more modern building formerly housing the Judicial, and today volunteers visit both there and in two other municipal jails in other parts of the city.

The mental hospital visits also started about the same time and follow much the same routine, except that the different setup there means the visitors can often pray with individual inmates in their own cells.

In the mid-1980s the community ran a ministry to juvenile delinquents in Juarez, but that was cut off by a change in the municipal government. A group of fifteen delinquents, some of them killers, lived for a time at a remote ranch called Los Jardines de Dios (God's Gardens) west of Juarez. Sergio Conde, a leading member of the community on the Juarez side, says thirteen of the fifteen ended up as law-abiding citizens.

## CHAPTER 3: THE MINISTRIES TODAY

The intention of this chapter is to get a handle on OLYC and its ministries as they operate today. Father Thomas thought that was a pretty funny idea, because "getting a handle" is exactly how OLYC *doesn't* operate. Hardly a day goes by that OLYC workers don't end up doing something they hadn't planned, or putting something they did plan on hold until a later time. Or canceling their plans altogether, if that's what God seems to want. "The human mind may devise many plans," says Prov. 19:21, "but it is the purpose of the LORD that will be established."

"When you get a handle on it, you let me know," Father Thomas laughed when the question was put to him that way.

All the same, a book like this has to paint some sort of overall picture, so here it is. We'll start with OLYC itself. Our Lady's Youth Center was founded in 1953, eleven years before Father Thomas arrived in El Paso. It is organized as a non-profit corporation with a board of directors which has often included non-Catholics; for legal reasons the community-based board was turned into an advisory board in 2001, with a new governing board appointed, consisting of Father Thomas and four of his closest associates. Following Father Thomas's death two other community members were added to the board. Ellen Hogarty is president.

OLYC is obedient to not one but four bishops (El Paso and Las Cruces on the American side and Juarez and Nuevo Casas Grandes in Mexico) because of the community's wide area of operations. Father Thomas himself was also obedient to his Jesuit provincial, based in New Orleans, as will be any future Jesuit assigned to the community. But the bishops and the provincial seldom interfere and have allowed the ministries great freedom.

So who does run the ministries? As much as possible, the people who actually do them. Catholic theologians call this "subsidiarity of function," keeping decision-making at as low a level as possible. "That person [in the ministry] knows more than anybody else, so they make the decision," Father Thomas said. "It doesn't go any higher up the ladder unless there's a need and they can't handle it." In fact, Father Thomas didn't necessarily even hear about the decisions. When interviewed at one point, for example, he wasn't able to say what was currently happening on the Jardines de Dios land (see Chapter 2), and had to refer questions to Sergio Conde.

Decisions involving more than one ministry are currently supervised by the same long-time community members who now make up the OLYC board—all U.S. residents at the moment. The supervisory role has been handled in various ways in the past, sometimes by a larger group including Juarez residents, but it changes in response to changing circumstances, including individuals' circumstances. In the last decade of his life Father Thomas was the only priest heavily involved in the ministries, although there have been several others over the years, including Father Sam Rosales, S.J. who worked with Father Thomas from 1980 to 1992 and again with the community for about two years following Father Thomas's death.

There is no question at all that Richard Thomas was the big gun in the community during his lifetime. Everybody looked to him for leadership, both in teaching and in example. But his official authority, in either Church or civil law, was pretty well zero. He didn't have an appointment as a pastor, which meant he couldn't even baptize or perform weddings without some local pastor's permission. He didn't have any paid employees, so he couldn't give orders on that basis. Decisions were, and still are, discussed and prayed over rather than coming down a chain of command.

"I don't have any authority except what people give me," Father Thomas said. "People look to me for leadership, but I don't meddle. Forty-plus years [in El Paso] gives me a lot of experience which other people don't have, and being a priest gives me some authority with Catholics. But we're submitted to one another, a mutual submission in love [Gal. 5:13c, Eph. 5:21]. We're anything but dictatorial."

The financial end of the operation is easier to describe. God provides the money, through unsolicited or barely-solicited donations, and the OLYC people spend it on His projects. There's no fundraising. Most OLYC services and items like tapes or sacramentals are given away for free. Father Thomas wouldn't accept Mass stipends or speaker's fees. The monthly OLYC newsletter does include a donation envelope, but the newsletter only goes to people who asked for it in the first place—760 recipients at present in the U.S.—and it never explicitly appeals for funds.

Expenditures are pretty much cash and carry. The community has never had a mortgage, even for Las Alas, and never goes into debt; it does run accounts at its major suppliers, for the sake of convenience, but always pays the bills on time. And if the community decides that God is calling it to a new ministry, it goes ahead on the assumption that God will provide the funds. So far, He always has.

"We've never run out of money," says Ellen Hogarty, "and if it slows down we feel God is telling us we're doing something He doesn't want to fund. Once we get the right message, the funds go back up."

Here's a rough overview of the OLYC ministries as they stood at this writing:

## LAS ALAS

Las Alas, the former department store a few blocks north of the old OLYC building, serves as office and storage space, staging area for the ministries' trips to Juarez, and site of a Wednesday evening prayer meeting with Mass and special classes for children and teens. An inner healing ministry takes place on Monday afternoons. Michael Reuter, office manager for Las Alas ("or I could put janitor, or food purchaser"), uses the facility for a two-year-long confirmation class for teenagers. First Communion classes are held weekly. Occasionally Reuter leads the seven-week Life in the Spirit seminar, the standard initiation to the charismatic renewal. The building is also used for special events.

Las Alas is not a parish church, and out of respect for nearby parishes, there is no Mass on Sunday; community members attend Sunday Mass in their home parishes, or at the Lord's Ranch. Reuter's confirmation students must be confirmed in local parishes, and first Communion is celebrated at Sacred Heart Church nearby.

## THE LORD'S RANCH

Since the end of farming, the Lord's Ranch has been used for mission trips and youth activities. It is also home to Mary Ann Halloran, her husband, Mike, who is ranch manager, and their children; several other community members; and a stream of long- and short-term visitors from all over the world.

Life on the ranch is simple and relaxed. Some of the residents live in small houses, while other residents and guests stay in simple bedrooms or dormitories in one of two larger buildings. For many years Father Thomas lived in a concrete-floored room in the men's dorm, a room which also served as his office; in 2001, at the community's urging, he moved to more private quarters to have more time for prayer and study.

To help identify with the poor of Juarez, who have trouble getting enough water, residents and visitors are

45

limited to two showers a week, even in the summer when the thermometer hits the hundred mark almost every day. (However, there is a no-frills outdoor swimming pool that's available at all hours during the summer.) And when some of the flush toilets started causing problems around 1989, they were replaced with outhouses.

"We take it very seriously that the money that comes in is the money given for the poor," says Ellen Hogarty. "We're living on it, so we try to keep it simple and be good stewards."

The social center of the ranch is a simple dining room in the other dorm building, furnished with picnic tables and benches and used for Mass, group Bible study, meals (mostly do-it-yourself) and general hanging around. There's no alcohol on the ranch, and smokers have to step well outside. There's no television, either, or secular music.

Bellarmine Hall, a new 9,000-square-foot event center funded by an anonymous donor, is now almost complete at the ranch. The center will provide more room for visiting groups, while also adding a new adoration chapel and dining room. Conditions for visitors will still be spartan—mattresses on the floor—but there will be flush toilets and showers.

The ranch is especially popular with high school and college groups during spring break and the summer, and some have been turned away due to lack of space. "They write now a year in advance," says Hogarty. "We fill up."

Since 1992 the ranch has also been home to the 50-kilowatt short wave radio station KJES. The call letters stand for King Jesus. The station broadcasts Scripture readings 7½ hours a day, in English and Spanish, pointed toward various parts of the world as dictated by a schedule. Listeners have contacted the station from as far away as China and New Zealand. Readers (frequently children) are never identified, and there is never a request for money.

## FOOD BANK AND CLINIC IN JUAREZ

The food bank operates mainly on the mesa in west Juarez, with a second distribution point at a church in Colonia Felipe Angeles, in a more crowded neighborhood about three miles away. The Monday food distribution at the mesa includes a prayer meeting and Mass. About a hundred families currently receive food, most of them people who kept coming to the prayer meeting when the food distribution was curtailed temporarily after the 1993 lawsuit. Maria Guzman and Pedro Ibarra, both Juarez residents, co-chair the operation.

The clinic carries on each Tuesday, with thirty to forty patients a week. Volunteer doctors and a rotation of volunteer dentists serve the patients. Jovita Nevarez arrives early with a prayer team, and patients must pray for healing and repent of sin before they see the doctor: the order laid down for the sick in Sir.[1] 38: 9-12 (see also Chapter 7).

---

[1] Sirach (sometimes called Ecclesiasticus) is a book contained in the Old Testament of Catholic Bibles, but listed as part of the Apocrypha or omitted altogether in Protestant Bibles.

"We stress that God is the one who heals us," says Aurora Alvarado, an El Paso nurse who is the clinic's chief organizer. "They cannot come into the clinic if they don't have prayer. We have had some people who have been very, very sick, and they are healed before they get into the clinic."

Cost is fifteen pesos (about $1.50 U.S.) for most treatments. At both medical and dental clinics, those who can't pay are treated for free. Medicine is also free, and the clinic pays for hospital care for high-risk pregnancies. In addition, about seventy mothers come each week for canned milk, cereal, oranges, and brownies for the children.

The community also operates a kindergarten on the mesa, with seventy pupils and seven teachers.

Each Friday there's another prayer meeting, and the mesa is headquarters for mobile food distribution, led by Jim Gallagher and Armando and Ramona Solano. Five or six teams of volunteers in vans visit about sixty-five individuals and families, many of them longtime recipients who have gotten too frail to make it to the food bank. The volunteers deliver boxes of food and pray with the people.

Meanwhile, the OLYC community has begun working in an even poorer neighborhood, Loma Blanca, in southeast Juarez. Marcos Nieblas of Juarez and a dozen volunteers have conducted a house-to-house census of need, and provide food and clothing. A Protestant church group which co-operates with OLYC has been building houses in the neighborhood, but the OLYC group helps with interior work and donates needed building materials. A warehouse is currently under construction for storage of food and building supplies, and to provide space for classes.

## JAIL AND MENTAL HOSPITAL MINISTRIES

About three dozen people visit the jails and mental hospital each Wednesday, in two separate teams because one of the jails is distant from the other locations. They pray first, then go in and minister to the inmates, and increasingly also to guards and other employees. The distant jail is also a high-security headquarters for a number of government agencies, including three levels of police, and the people there have been open to prayer ministry lately—at least partly because they run a constant risk of being killed by drug dealers. The volunteers are even allowed to interrupt classes of police cadets for preaching and prayer. Anita Osuna leads the visits to the centrally-located jails, Marcos Nieblas the ministry to the other jail.

## THE DUMP MINISTRY

Most people in the OLYC community still talk about "the dump" when they mean the area where the Christmas multiplication took place in 1972, but the actual dump operation has been gone from the site since 1994 and the people who actually work there prefer the neighborhood's new official name, Colonia Lomas de Morelos. The operation is now based in a cement block building. Programs over the years have included a food store, a school, cut-rate medical, dental and optical clinics, a day care center, and a children's dining room.

The operation is now separately organized as Centro Communitario del Espiritu Santo, with its own board of directors and its own fundraising. The prayer meeting at Las Alas still takes a collection at the door for the ministry.

## MISCELLANEOUS

The community operates a pro-life ministry which provides clothing, shelter and other services, including midwives, for women with problem pregnancies. Volunteers like Gabriela Federico also give pro-life talks to youngsters in the classes at Las Alas, to visiting groups at the ranch, and in local Catholic schools and other locations. Delia Ramos and Jovita Nevarez provide post-abortion ministry to about 50 women a year, leading a nine-week prayer program followed by a group retreat to allow God to free the women from guilt. Some of these women are looking for healing years or decades after their abortions, but as the ministry becomes better known, more women who have had abortions recently are coming. Ramos also speaks about post-abortion healing during pro-life presentations to visiting groups, especially student groups, out of sensitivity to the fact that such groups often include young women who have already had an abortion.

Until his death Father Thomas led a "Young Shepherds" program in which about a dozen high school and college women were trained for one-on-one ministry to other youngsters as well as for evangelism and Christian witness in the schools. He met weekly with the group, providing intensive spiritual training including the Ignatian principles of his own Jesuit background, and was astonished by the results.

"They're tough and they're effective," he said. "They can do in a few minutes what an adult can't do at all. And they're highly self-motivated. They come up with a lot of stuff on their own, and I hear about it later." Ellen Hogarty has now taken over the leadership of the Young Shepherds.

The community has recently resumed a former practice of praying during rock concerts, events OLYC volunteers strongly oppose. (If you want to know why, see Chapter 10.) In earlier days, volunteers prayed in a rented building near the El Paso Coliseum, the site of many concerts. The result, Father Thomas said, was electrical problems and other foul-ups for the bands. "Word got around that El Paso wasn't a good place to play—something always goes wrong." Today, volunteers pray at Las Alas and in cars and vans parked near concert sites, because the building is no longer available. Prayer runs in shifts from 5 to 11 p.m. Formerly prayer ended at 9, but then the volunteers learned that one concert finally got under way just after prayer ended.

Los Jardines de Dios, in a remote location west of Juarez, is currently running as a farm with two workers, supervised by Sergio and Lucia Conde. The community is holding on to the site in case it can be used again in the future, for a juvenile delinquent ministry or for some other purpose.

# CHAPTER 4: THE PEOPLE OF OLYC

When Norma Garcia was twenty-two, she was a city council member in her home town and working full-time supervising health workers.

At thirty, she's out of both politics and the paid workforce, living at the Lord's Ranch and volunteering full-time in OLYC ministries. She has no trouble deciding which life she likes better.

Raised as a practicing Catholic, Garcia had stopped going to church around age seventeen. Talented and likeable, she organized a teen pregnancy prevention program and drew the attention of a political faction in her home town, the El Paso suburb of Sunland Park, New Mexico. She was asked to run for office, and she won.

But within months, her life turned sour. Political battles spilled over into serious legal trouble, including a state investigation, and her day job was threatened by funding cutbacks. She had been struggling with depression and thoughts of suicide, and the pressures made her worse.

After she had tried everything else—counseling, psychiatry, prescription drugs—her aunt took her to

Sunday Mass at the ranch. Father Thomas kept looking at her through Mass, and when she asked to see him afterwards, "he said 'sure!', like he was my long-time friend." Only later did she learn that he didn't normally counsel on Sundays at that time.

She went to confession ("he told me one of my sins, which really surprised me. I thought, do I have it written somewhere on me?"), and then to inner healing with Mary Ann Halloran and Ellen Hogarty. Back on her emotional feet within weeks, she began to volunteer in the ministries, and also took a trip to Medjugorje, site of reported apparitions of the Virgin Mary. Father Thomas prayed about her legal problems and told her not to bother hiring a lawyer, because the problems would blow over. They did.

Uncertain of God's plans for her future, she considered joining a convent—"I thought the ranch was too holy for me"—and assumed the first step would be quitting city council, but God seemed to be saying "no." "I thought, surely He doesn't want me to leave my full-time job," she recalls, but when she prayed for guidance one lunchtime before the Blessed Sacrament, "God said 'I already told you to leave that job.' He told me to stay in politics until I finished my term."

She quit her day job in 2003 and her council term ended in March 2006. Since then she has lived full-time at the ranch. At various times she has been co-leader of the Friday food bank ministry, worked in the jail ministry and the radio station, and served as "welcoming committee" for girls and young women who come to stay at the ranch.

"I've seen girls who were fallen-away Catholics turn back to God, turn their lives around and decide to serve Him," she says. "I've seen that in young men as well. It happens after one weekend here, or a week, or whatever.

"You really feel you're living the Gospel here. It's complete abandonment to divine providence. They're really living out what the Word of God says."

She also discerned a vocation for marriage and motherhood. How could she meet a husband? "I don't feel like I'm living in a convent or anything like that," she said when first interviewed in April 2006. "I'm constantly meeting people. God has a plan for me. I don't know how He's going to work it out, but He's going to come through.

"I know I'm in the right place."

And so she was. Fellow ranch resident Michael Reuter, after waiting long enough to feel confident that Garcia, too, was called to the life of the community, asked her on New Year's Eve of 2006 if she would begin courtship with him. They were engaged on Holy Saturday of 2007 and married in October of that year.

It's just as hard to get a handle on the people of the OLYC community as it is to get a handle on the ministries. For one thing, nobody really knows how many people *belong* to the community. It depends partly on how you define "belong," of course, but even given a definition, there's no precise way of coming up with a number. Going by rough counts of how many people actually work in the ministries (in other words, not just attending the prayer meeting or receiving services), Michael Reuter tallies up a total somewhere around 75 on the El Paso side of the river. Nobody can provide even that close an estimate for the Juarez side, but from piecing together conversations with the leaders of the ministries there, it looks as if another 75 or so would be a good guess.

But when it comes to describing the community, numbers are the least of the problem. What's really hard to get a handle on is the way the community lives. Is it easy? Sure, anybody could do it. Is it difficult? So difficult hardly anybody would be willing to go the whole route.

From the point of view of formal control or day-to-day hardship, everything is almost totally free and relaxed. It's nothing like a cult; in fact, it isn't even a "covenant community" of the type that used to be popular in the early days of the charismatic renewal. There's no membership register, and if there were it would have to be updated constantly because of the number of people coming and going. Most people in the community live in their own homes, and nobody supervises anybody's private life, or tries to stop anybody from leaving for any reason.

"It's like a school of fish," Father Thomas said. "You get some joining and some leaving, but the school goes on. If somebody is around and participates wholeheartedly and wants to continue to be around, they're accepted on that basis if they're living a clean life.

"Anybody that's going to participate in a ministry, we expect to be very obedient to the leader of that ministry. A lot of the stuff we do is delicate. But what they do at home, we don't know, we don't ask, we don't meddle. If they're living in flagrant sin, that disqualifies them, but if they're living in flagrant sin they won't want to be here anyway."

Another nice touch, a big surprise for visitors from the secular world, is that nobody ever seems to be in a hurry. The whole atmosphere is relaxed. People work hard, but there's always plenty of free time, not only for prayer but for leisure. There's lots of earnestness, but also lots of laughter and affectionate teasing and even practical jokes.

But it's only the rules and the atmosphere that are easygoing. Expectations are a whole different story. Community members are expected to embrace the cross, in little ways and in big ways. Not everybody in the community meets all those expectations, but nobody can avoid hearing about them.

On the small end of the scale, the leaders are dead against certain things many people would see as routine and harmless. Like popular music, country as well as rock. And superstitions—even something as ordinary as crossing your fingers for luck. Drinking, smoking and television are discouraged. None of this is enforced, except at the ranch or during community activities, but the message gets across clearly all the same.

Bigger than any of that, and a lot harder to avoid, is a certain surrender of will—not across the board, but in a few key areas, just enough to separate those who mean it from those who don't. Newcomers, especially, tend to be given assignments they wouldn't have chosen for themselves. OLYC's work has gotten a fair bit of publicity over the years, both locally and internationally, and the community sometimes attracts visitors or prospective volunteers with too much personal agenda and not enough personal commitment. But there are ways of sorting them out—"you can expect to be challenged spiritually during your time here," say the visitors' guidelines at the Lord's Ranch—and those who don't get with the program in a hurry don't last.

For example: the day I arrived on my first visit to OLYC, within 10 minutes in fact, I was put to work ripping hundreds of pharmaceutical samples out of their tiny one-pill plastic containers and sorting them into jars for use at the food bank clinic. The second day I was up at 5 a.m. on a winter morning to visit the food bank, where I helped dig a ditch in ankle-deep mud. The third day I was sent on the Juarez jail ministry, locked in the cells with 20 prisoners and just three other volunteers, none of whom spoke English. People who come looking for spiritual direction are also given an assignment, maybe reading some Bible passages or listening to a tape, and if they don't do it, Father Thomas said, "we just wait until they're serious before spending more time with them." Even Reuter's teenage confirmation students have to promise not to date for the whole two-year program.

But the biggest expectation of all is the one that surprised Norma Garcia: giving up all concern for making a living. God has promised to provide (Luke 12:22-34, the lilies of the field). Give freely whatever you have to offer, and God will take care of you. The majority of people don't do that, of course, even within the community, but it remains the ultimate goal, subject to discernment and God's guidance (see Chapter 12), and over time more and more people are doing it.

"I'm always asking people to come work full-time for the Lord," Father Thomas said. "They say 'Who's going to pay the bills?' I say God will pay the bills."

Here are a few more OLYC people, just a sample from among the many who might be profiled:

**SERGIO CONDE VARELA** was a hotshot Juarez lawyer, rector of the local university, and a city official in charge of tax collection when he first ran into OLYC in 1974. The store at the dump was operating without a permit, and Conde had three of the leaders hauled into his office to explain themselves.

"I wanted to send them to jail for a little while," he says.

But the three prayed silently in tongues (so he found out later) while he was questioning them, and suddenly he couldn't crack down on them the way he had intended.

The following year his wife, **LUCIA**, began attending prayer meetings, and Sergio followed. The year after that, he quit his secular jobs to become store manager at the dump, and the couple gave away their money and possessions.

"The Bible says he who lives by the Gospel will have 101 per cent now, and afterward eternal life" (Mark 10:29f, loosely quoted via a translator), Sergio says. "I thought, I'm going to try that. I came to zero in my bank accounts. It was a difficult life, but God gave me the ability to live it."

In 1983 a new Juarez mayor was elected. The new mayor, Francisco Barrio, was not from Sergio's political party, but he was a devout Catholic, and he invited Sergio to serve as his number two man. That gave Sergio a chance to clean up the municipal jail and abolish torture, while Lucia played a key role in founding the juvenile delinquent ministry (see Chapter 2). This foray into politics ended at the next election, and Sergio went back to the dump. Now he works as a lawyer for the community and for the poor living near Jardines de Dios, and he and Lucia manage the Jardines property. They also give occasional teachings at the prayer meetings at Las Alas.

**HECTOR and MARY BENCOMO** of El Paso have an even more complicated story to tell. Hector, a former El Paso city council member, has actually been involved with OLYC longer than Father Thomas—he was on the board of directors in the early 60s. But that didn't give him any particular head start.

"I didn't take it that seriously," he says. "I was a very poor Catholic, a poor Christian. I was a politician, a businessman, and that's where my heart was." He was also a super-controlling husband, an alcohol and drug abuser and a big-time bar brawler. "Eat well, drink well and beat the heck out of somebody—that made a successful night." And none of that changed very much even when he was baptized in the Holy Spirit around 1970. Even when he got involved in the OLYC jail ministry and started leading Marriage Encounter. Even when he was healed of tuberculosis and a heart attack. "The Lord would knock me down and I'd get back up and do the same thing," he says. "I couldn't give up my drinking, my friends, my business, my politics. I was really trying to commit suicide, and I wouldn't admit it."

About 1990, at around age 60, he left the community for a long bender on booze and marijuana. Mary left him, but she didn't stop praying for him. "It was war," she says now. "And he came back." Hector took his last drink on New Year's Eve, 1991.

Meanwhile, Mary had her own struggles with her marriage and with physical and psychological illness. At her first OLYC prayer meeting, about 1980, Hector had to help her up the stairs. But not long after, she was taken to the food bank and put in the prayer room with the "abuelitas" (Mexican grandmothers) who pray for the other workers.

"I walked into that little room and it was just like heaven," she recalls. "When they prayed for me I saw Jesus, and He was all love. There was a bright light – I could cover my eyes with my hands and it was still there. It lasted for days, and I felt love for the first time in many years." That same first day, she was healed of hypoglycemia so severe the symptoms resembled a nervous breakdown; she drank a huge Coke with no bad effects and she gave up the pills she had been taking by the handful.

Mary has done a variety of jobs with the community over the years, holding major responsibilities at the food bank, jail and mental hospital. Now she takes care of altar linens and vestments, and prays at the ranch.

Until stepping down recently due to ill health, Hector led a Monday food distribution and worked at KJES. But his favorite ministry was always the jail. He visited all three municipal jails each week, preaching and handing out rosaries and miraculous medals to the guards and officials, and medals to the prisoners, who aren't allowed to have rosaries. He always mentioned his drinking problems. "It helps me in the jail ministry," he said. "I don't see any difference between myself and those guys. I want to transmit that same love of Jesus to them, so that they can say 'Lord, help me to change my life.'"

Twenty-plus years ago, **JIM GALLAGHER**'s life was in an uproar. Today he'd say the trouble was his own sinful lifestyle, but as he saw it at the time, his problems were job pressures and his wife. The solution, he decided, was to leave his wife, **KEITH**, for another woman.

But God had different plans, and so did Gallagher's law partner and friend of 30 years, **RICHARD MUNZINGER**, a longtime member of the OLYC community. The two lawyers had adjoining offices in the firm where they worked, and when Gallagher finally got up the courage to tell Munzinger his plans, Munzinger laid down the law. "That's Satan's plan to destroy you and your family," he said. "Don't let it happen!" His words pulled Gallagher up short; the two men knelt right in the office and prayed, and Gallagher decided to break off the extramarital affair immediately and ask his wife's forgiveness.

The Gallaghers still had a long struggle ahead, but God was at work. They found help for their marriage, and also for their concerns about the direction of the non-Catholic church in which they were both active. Munzinger invited them to the Lord's Ranch, and if Munzinger had been plain-spoken, Father Thomas's teachings were pure revelation. "He spoke God's truth undiluted, uncompromised," Jim recalls. "Those Scriptures that make you uncomfortable, he'd tear a hole in you, and then widen the hole."

In search of truth, but without a church home in the early 90s, the Gallaghers shared time between the Catholic church through Father Thomas and the Episcopal church. Their marriage was healed, through Father Thomas's counseling, Keith's constant prayer, and a non-denominational marriage course. In 1991 Jim had a life-changing experience at an Episcopalian charismatic conference in Denver, but the call to the Catholic Church grew stronger due not only to Father Thomas's homilies but also to his lifestyle and that of the whole OLYC community. "They lived the Gospel," Jim recalls.

Jim and Keith accompanied Father Thomas in 1995 on a mission trip to Ireland, still as non-Catholics. A few months later they were received into the Catholic Church at the ranch, Father Thomas's first and only confirmations under permission newly-granted by Bishop Ramirez. "Our RCIA was to meet with Father Thomas for an hour or two after Mass," Jim says. "He answered all our questions."

About 1997 Jim went on an Ignatian retreat in Memphis, nearly a month long, and discerned that God was calling him to get out of his 34-year law practice.

He logged his last billable hour in 2000. Keith continues to work part-time on private bookkeeping jobs.

Today Jim co-leads the Friday food ministry, is part of the prayer team Tuesdays at the clinic, and visits the jails and mental hospital in Juarez if his other duties permit. He has become point man for unusual medical and monetary needs of the poor, with financial backing from the St. Vincent de Paul Society in El Paso and his contacts from years of defending doctors and hospitals in litigation. Often this also means getting humanitarian permits for Juarez residents to cross the border for treatment by El Paso doctors and hospitals.

Both Gallaghers sometimes teach at the Wednesday prayer meetings, and together they have made a ministry out of their own healed marriage. They meet with couples in need and they also teach Catholic truths in a course, Married God's Way, designed for stale or troubled marriages, or just good marriages that want to get better.

"God speaks to us in many ways, if we let Him," says Jim. "Once you've been blessed by Jesus, it's awfully hard to say no. We're just so blessed in what little we do."

You'll be sure to spot **FRANCISCA TERRAZAS** at the prayer meetings at Las Alas. She's the one picking out partners to dance with her in the conga line—young people, visiting priests, aging writers from Canada. She leads, they follow, even when she has to spin somebody a foot taller than she is.

Meanwhile, her younger sister **BLASA CORONA**, whose own high spirits lean more toward wisecracks, is cheerfully chugging away in the same conga line despite her "two flat tires"—the knee replacement and the broken thigh that she has had in recent years.

The sisters, aged 81 and 78, are among the hardest members of the OLYC community to miss, especially if you happen to be at the Lord's Ranch on a day when they come to cook a lunch that would put a restaurant to shame. Born in Durango, Mexico, they have both lived in the United States since the 1950s, and they've been around OLYC since the mid-80s.

It all began when both sisters visited a Eucharistic conference in the El Paso Civic Center. Blasa went to just one Mass and found herself in tears—to her total annoyance. All the same, she decided to check out a Life in the Spirit seminar at a local convent soon after, and learned more than she was even aware of not knowing.

"I didn't know anything about Jesus," she recalls. "I knew about Mary and God, but I didn't have Jesus in my heart."

She got her answer, though. She seemed to have the gift of tongues, and she was sent to Father Thomas, who was more experienced than the seminar leaders, to discern whether her tongue was from God. She got lost looking for the old OLYC building, but finally she found her way in.

"I thought, I'm staying here forever. I love it," she says. "I found peace. God loved me very much. I felt like something embraced me and touched me. I laughed, I

65

cried, I danced like crazy. I didn't know anybody, but I felt like I knew everybody."

Francisca stayed for the whole Eucharistic conference, but she was a bit slower to get to the Life in the Spirit seminar. Finally she went, looking for a closer personal encounter with a God she mainly knew intellectually. Soon she, too, was at OLYC.

The sisters did a variety of chores around OLYC, and later the Lord's Ranch. Francisca even milked cows, a skill she had learned back in Durango. Francisca was also the first to get involved on the Juarez side, going with Mary Bencomo to wash clothes and clean houses for the sick and elderly. In the late 80s the sisters drove around Juarez together picking children up from the four points of the compass for the weekly children's Mass; during the Mass they patrolled outside with baseball bats to keep the local cholos (young toughs) from disrupting the liturgy,

Once the woman who prepared the altar went on vacation and asked Blasa to fill in for her. Blasa had no idea how to do that. She pointed out that other people could do a better job, but the woman insisted. So Blasa went off to the store when her ride to Juarez was due that week, still hoping to get out of the job. It didn't work; the driver made a second pass by her house just as she was returning home. "I felt like Jonah," she says. The altar work went fine.

For nine years the sisters were in charge of food delivery in Juarez, at first going twice a week and doing it all themselves, later heading the Friday ministry with other people helping. They stepped down three years ago.

"When we go to visit these people, we think we're giving something, but we're receiving more," says Blasa.

**DELIA RAMOS** did not start out as a member of the Rick Thomas fan club. And she had plenty of reason for that.

The first time she saw Father Thomas, his picture was in the newspaper as part of a group of pro-lifers. Early in her marriage, she had had two abortions of her own, abortions she didn't want, and with serious complications that left her in the hospital, close to death. The newspaper picture hit her like a slap in the face.

"I got very upset," she recalls. "It was the first time in many years I got in touch with my abortions. Being in the hospital had been a good excuse not to think about it.

"I was angry at that priest. I decided I was pro-choice, because nobody else can know about a woman's situation."

Born in Chihuahua, Mexico, to a well-off family, Ramos had come to El Paso with her own family in 1986, and she and her husband opened a successful business. But Ramos was not a happy woman, demanding too much of her two sons—"I wanted them to be perfect"—and showing her sadness in other ways. In the early 90s, a woman who came by the business to sell tamales began to invite her to a place where she would feel good, and finally asked for a ride for herself.

The place was the old OLYC, and the occasion was a prayer meeting. Ramos grudgingly agreed: she didn't like parking her car in the questionable neighborhood, she wouldn't hang around for the full two hours, and she would only stand in the doorway while the tamale woman attended the meeting. "I thought I was a very conventional Catholic and I didn't like the people singing and clapping and dancing."

Finally the woman left town, and Ramos was relieved—no more prayer meetings. Then another woman asked for a ride to see a certain priest at the OLYC address. Guess who.

Ramos didn't think there was any priest at OLYC, but she agreed to take the woman, and this time she went on in to the prayer meeting and even started dancing— until she saw another dancer, Father Thomas himself. "I was so mad. I couldn't stand him, so I left." But with no reason and no invitation, she found herself returning to the next meeting, and worse yet, stuck sitting uncomfortably next to Father Thomas in the only seat available. After six months or so of this, Ellen Hogarty invited women to volunteer for pro-life work. Ramos signed up, and found herself working with a troubled pregnant woman.

"It was a very healing experience for me," she says. "I felt I was giving life to my babies that I didn't have."

She had separated from her husband by then, but still worked in the business. When the pregnant woman's child was born, in 1996, Ramos felt a call from God to full-time pro-life work. Father Thomas, by now her friend, prayed that God would open or close doors to show her the way, and soon she left the business, with her sons' approval, and committed herself to the pro-life ministry full-time.

She had a bit of savings and didn't lose her house, but it wasn't easy. Some of her friends abandoned her, and money was tight, especially for a woman used to having money. But every time she was tempted to go back to paid work, money would come from somewhere, unsolicited. "The Lord provided for my needs. I didn't choose to come and work for God—God brought me to Him. I'm very sure that I'm where He wants me to be." She says her sons have both turned out well, and her relationship with them is good. They don't seem to remember the bad parts of their childhood. "God raised them," she says, "because I wasn't able."

Early on, her pro-life work meant letting pregnant women stay at her house, but she didn't feel that was good enough. She now supervises apartments which a donor has provided to the community for the women's use. Meanwhile, she and **JOVITA NEVAREZ** see about 50 women a year for a post-abortion healing program, praying through the whole experience over nine weeks and then holding a group retreat "to turn the page and start a new life."

"Guilt is one of the worst things we face," she says. "We can't free ourselves. Women who have had abortions feel that God is there, but we are not allowed to approach Him because we are out of God's love. We focus on how God has always been there for them. From the first visit, you can see how much their faces have changed."

For women who haven't had an abortion, she says, "it's better to have your kid than not to have it. You're always going to regret [abortion]. It [having the baby] isn't easy, of course, but it's better long-term." And for those who have had an abortion, she gives the advice God gave Lot's wife: "do not look back." (Gen. 19:17)

"I don't want to be a pillar of salt," she says. "I don't want to look back. That's a Scripture that's very powerful for me."

When **TOMMY** and **CECI BARRIENTOS** first came to an OLYC prayer meeting at a time of personal crisis, they had very different reactions.

Tommy wanted to go home. Ceci knew she had come home.

Tommy, from Zacatecas in Mexico, and Ceci, born in El Paso, met and married in Los Angeles, where Ceci was raised. They moved back to El Paso and opened a restaurant downtown. They were Catholics, but all that meant was going to Sunday Mass. "We were very ambitious, very much in the world," says Ceci.

In 1993, though, their marriage was in difficulty, and they accepted an invitation to attend a prayer meeting at the OLYC building with a friend.

"She had invited us before, but we never paid attention," says Tommy. This time, he decided it was worth a try – "I was searching for something, but I didn't know what."

At first glance, this wasn't it. Tommy had never seen charismatic worship before, "and when I saw people dancing, I wanted to get out of there in a hurry." He stayed only because he didn't want to hurt their friend's feelings.

Ceci, on the other hand, stayed because she wanted to stay. She had had a charismatic experience of Jesus in Los Angeles, at age 13; she had drifted away, but "when I walked into the old Youth Center, I knew I was back."

Tommy didn't go back the next week, but he did go to buy supplies for the restaurant at a local store, and who should he meet there but a woman from the prayer meeting. "She kept me there for like an hour, explaining this stuff." He decided to go back one more time, the following week, just to observe. Mary Ann Halloran and Ellen Hogarty were leading the music. "I just kept my head down. But when I started listening to the songs, they just broke me. My heart started pounding. That was the door... they were making me cry.

"By the end of the prayer meeting I decided I had to go back."

They talked with Father Thomas, who challenged them to work for the Lord, but with their children still at home, they were afraid to give up the restaurant.

"Father said, 'don't worry about it,'" Tommy says. "'You have your ministry there. Just pray to the Lord about how you can serve him in that place.'"

Walk into the restaurant today, and you'll see what the Lord told them. The restaurant is plastered with Christian posters and literature—Bible verses, calls to feed the poor, pro-life messages. But that's only the visible part. While Ceci and Tommy continue to run the restaurant as a business, they often feed OLYC workers or poor people for free, and pray, counsel or witness for customers when they get a chance. After hours, they have used the premises for Bible study for a men's group and for women from nearby government offices; they also pray for the government itself.

It hasn't always been easy—especially speaking out. "I was afraid people would never come back," says Tommy. At election time in particular, though they have no party allegiance, they're seen as Democrats because they're Hispanic, or Republicans (and traitors) because of their pro-life position; they have lost a few customers, and some of those customers leave hostile notes instead of tips.

But they also get support. People bring them money, furniture or clothes for the poor, says Ceci. One woman gave $20 or $30 cash but promised to return with a check, which Ceci thought would be about the same size. "It was $500," she says.

They also belong to a prayer group of about 10 couples which meets Friday nights for two hours of prayer from Scripture. "God will show you spiritual things that you've never imagined through this prayer," says Tommy.

"I've never been so happy in my life, and so free."

**MICHAEL REUTER** was a 19-year-old heavy metal fan and backslidden Catholic in North Dakota when a college classmate asked him where he'd go if he died that night. "I had enough catechism that I said 'I'd go straight to hell,'" he says now. "To hear those words come out of my own lips really shocked me."

He scrapped his records and rock paraphernalia and started praying a lot, and soon he saw *Viva Cristo Rey*, a video about OLYC, at a showing in his home parish. "Boom! All the pieces snapped together in my mind," he says. He met Father Thomas, who was visiting North Dakota, soon after, and in 1985 Reuter came to El Paso. His original intention was to stay a year and then become a priest, but he never left.

"I believe this is God's perfect will for me," he says. His special joy is youth work, at the prayer meetings or on retreats at the ranch. "Kids come in, they're 18 and they look like 40," he says. "Then they attend for a few weeks, and the youth comes back. They're a new creation (2 Cor. 5:17). It's so wonderful to see—how could you not say there's a God?"

From an early point in his time in the community he had also felt called to marriage, but couldn't imagine where he would find a wife to share such a radical lifestyle. After two decades, God provided an answer: Norma Garcia. "She was well worth the wait," he says.

**ELLEN HOGARTY**, raised in a charismatic Catholic family in Hawaii, first came to the Lord's Ranch in 1983, when she was 18. It was a three-week visit after her first year at Franciscan University in Steubenville, Ohio, and that was supposed to be that.

"But during the first week I was here I felt a really strong call to stay here," she says. "I didn't like that at all. My plan was to finish college. But after wrestling

73

with the Lord a while, I finally submitted my will to His, and then I was flooded with joy, and the surety that this was home." She got permission from her parents to stay the summer, then went back to Hawaii and told them God was calling her to the OLYC ministries. Her father gave his blessing right away; her mother argued against it for a while, but eventually came around. Hogarty has been in the community ever since, working first milking the cows and goats and pruning trees, then as bookkeeper, next as secretary, and now as president of the board. She has a strong gift of prophecy.

**MARY ANN HALLORAN**, from Phoenix, arrived at the ranch in 1976, one of the first people to inquire after reading about OLYC in *New Covenant* magazine. Her future husband, **MIKE**, turned up from Rhode Island two years later on what was supposed to be a brief visit. He had been a nominal Catholic all his life, but a short time earlier he had had a conversion experience, so he had given up his construction job and his recreational drugs, and he was looking for a way to serve God. "I came for two weeks and never left," he says. The Hallorans married in 1979 and have raised eight children on the ranch.

All the Halloran children have been educated at home. That was a family decision, not a community rule; other parents who have lived on the ranch in the past have sent their children to local schools. Home schooling doesn't mean social isolation, though. The Halloran youngsters have plenty of friends their own age, some through youth activities at Las Alas and some through the sports teams they play on. "Socialization with other kids is important, but they don't need six hours of it a day," says Mary Ann. "They're comfortable with adults, they're comfortable with kids."

From a visitor's perspective, it seems to work. On one of my earlier visits, **NATHAN**, 17 at the time, showed the social skills of a 25-year-old, and **PETER**, then 13, could have passed for 16. Nathan is now a Jesuit seminarian, studying for the priesthood and currently teaching at Jesuit High School in New Orleans.

Everybody has an individual story, but everybody also agrees that the real story at OLYC is a community story. The people, 150 or however many it is, do a better job together than they could do separately. "We're taught the Word of God here, and that it's to be put into practice," says Michael Reuter. "This is what God said, and this is what you do. When you gather people together who believe it that way, it becomes real."

"Reading Matthew 25 [vv 31-46, feeding the hungry, welcoming the stranger, caring for the sick, visiting the imprisoned], you'd wonder how you can do it all," says Mary Ann Halloran. "As community, you can."

Her husband makes a slightly different point.

"I need my brothers and sisters to call me to account," he says. "Away from here it would be easy to have a beer every night, and then it would be two, and then three, and then a couple of hours of television a night, and then there'd be dust on the Bible and I'd be a nominal Christian again, just going to church on Sunday.

"I need community to seriously follow the Lord. I stay here because I think my salvation depends on it."

Fr. Richard M. Thomas, S.J.
(Fr. Rick)

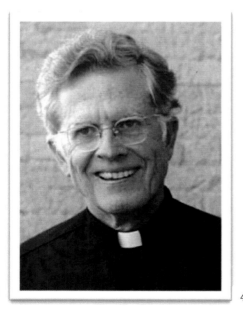

5

Christmas at the garbage dump in 1972 when
the first multiplication of food occurred.

6

7

Cardboard and pallet shacks near the Food Bank.

8

Frank Alarcon, who was present during the Christmas
multiplication of food at the garbage dump in Juarez, and who
later dedicated his life to helping the people there
(see page 21, 36).

9

Praying for and feeding the prisoners
during the jail ministry.

10

11

One of the many groups who have visited
the Lord's Ranch in Vado, New Mexico.

12

Las Alas – the large department store OLYC was "not
supposed to" have been able to acquire but which
now is its headquarters in El Paso, Texas.

13

The elderly enjoying a meal at the Food Bank in Juarez and the kitchen crew having fun serving it up.

14

15

Aurora Alvarado, the nurse who directs the Lord's Clinic at the Food Bank in Juarez (see page 48, 94).

16

Francisca Terrazas, left, and her sister Blasa Corona, who headed up the ministry to the homebound for many years (see page 64, 65).

Lucia & Sergio Conde Varela (see page 59)

Jovita Nevarez
(see page 47, 69)

Aurora Villa, who led the
Food Bank ministry for many
years until her death in 2007.

20

George Roberts (see page 119) delivering food (above) and Hector and Mary Bencomo (see page 60) ministering to patients at a mental hospital in Juarez (below).

21

22

Delia Ramos (see page 67)

23

Ellen Hogarty (see page 73)

24

The Halloran family (see page 74)

25

Tommy & Ceci Barrientos in their restaurant (see page 70).

26

The author, Richard Dunstan, visiting a home in Juarez.

27

Jim Gallagher (see page 62) and Norma Reuter preparing the food distribution routes at the Food Bank in Juarez.

28

Norma and Mike Reuter (see page 53,72) on honeymoon in Rome.

29

Father Thomas greeting the prisoners at the jail in Juarez, Mexico.

30

Catechism class for the children at Loma Blanca (see page 48).

31

International shortwave radio station KJES at the Lord's Ranch.

32

Chuy Salgado and his wife, Mirna. Chuy was healed of malignant tumor of the mouth (see page 95).

33

Bill & Marion Halloran with their grandson, Robby Delgado, who was healed of cancer of the eye (see page 100).

34

Children from the kindergarten at the Food Bank in Juarez.

Father Thomas celebrating Mass at Las Alas.

36

Father Thomas celebrated Mass up until the last two weeks of his life.

37

Mary Ann Halloran and Father Thomas touring the construction of Bellarmine Hall, a few months before Father's death in 2006.

# CHAPTER 5: MIGHTY WORKS OF GOD

One Saturday night about 1976, members of the dump workers' co-operative and the OLYC community were on the job at the Juarez dump site when a truck owned by the co-operative came rolling in with a load of fuel oil. In those days there were always embers smoldering in the trash, and as the truck arrived the wind shifted and the truck caught fire. The blaze spread quickly, fed by the oil and trash and cardboard on the ground. There was no water to put the fire out, no fire department to call, and no money to replace either the oil or the truck, so the people—about 30 of them—took the only option they had.

"We stood around the truck, held hands and prayed," says Sergio Conde, who was managing the dump store at the time. "In eight or 10 minutes the fire went out." The truck had no damage, except for some harmless scorching.

Sometime in the mid-1980s, as the OLYC team paid its weekly visit to the Juarez mental hospital, the volunteers met a young man named Saul on the sidewalk just outside the gate. Saul's mother and sister had brought him to be prayed for. He walked with a shuffle and could hardly speak at all. So the team circled around him and prayed.

"I had my hand on the back of his neck, and he began to shake like a leaf in a storm," says Richard Munzinger, the El Paso lawyer, who was with the team that day. The volunteers went on into the hospital, and Saul and his family were gone when they came out, but the next week Saul was back. He could talk a little now, but not much. The team prayed again.

"He shouted out 'gloria a Dios!' (glory to God) and started singing and praying," Munzinger recalls. "He sounded like a Mexican radio announcer, and two weeks earlier he couldn't speak."

One morning in 1997, a mother brought her eight-month-old baby son to the clinic at the mesa in west Juarez. The boy had been born with the frontal lobe of his skull sunken in. The bone was pressing on the brain, causing retardation. The child had the totally blank expression and lack of response that psychologists call "flat affect." "He didn't act like a little baby," says Aurora Alvarado, the clinic organizer. A neurosurgeon agreed to operate, but he said the surgery would be risky and wouldn't cure the existing retardation. The child was given vitamins for two or three weeks to get his strength up, and clinic volunteers prayed over him before and after the operation.

It was 15 months before the boy was seen at the clinic again. This time, there was nothing abnormal about him. "He was active, playing," says Alvarado. For some time afterward he continued to come to the clinic with his mother, who has a younger child. "He had no sign of mental retardation," Alvarado says.

In early 2005, Chuy Salgado, a Juarez engineer, was diagnosed by five different doctors with a rare and untreatable malignant tumor of the mouth. The most recent previous case known was found in China 30 years earlier. One doctor took Salgado and his wife, Mirna, to the Lord's Ranch for prayer.

"That prayer was answered," Mirna wrote in the July 2005 OLYC newsletter. "The doctor called, saying, 'Mrs. Salgado, undoubtedly there must have been many prayers said for your husband, and the Lord listened. The tumor is benign.'"

Over the years, reports of miracles have attracted more attention than anything else OLYC is doing, in a variety of magazine articles and in two books by Father Rene Laurentin in the 1980s—both with the word "miracle" in their titles. But miracles aren't nearly as important to the OLYC community itself as they are to outside observers. It almost seems as if the people at OLYC take miracles, or events that might be miracles, for granted; they have better things to do than to get miracles authenticated by Vatican commissions or outside skeptics, or even to sort them out for themselves.

"You have to define what you mean by a miracle," Father Thomas said. "People report miracles [here] all the time. I don't know how many of them would meet criteria, and I don't know what the criteria would be. People tell me about miracles, and I have no way of knowing whether it's true or not, or how miraculous it is.

"We're not equipped to document these things in any scientific way that would satisfy people who keep records. We can't keep track of anything."

"Miracle" is more of a popular term or a Church term than a biblical term anyway; *dunamis*, the Greek word that's sometimes translated "miracle" in the New Testament, is more correctly translated "mighty work" or "deed of power," and literally means simply "power" (e.g. Matt. 11: 21, 23; 1 Cor. 12:10). In John's Gospel, *semeion*, a Greek word meaning "sign," is used instead (e.g. John 2:11, the wedding at Cana). And miracles or no miracles, nobody at OLYC doubts that God has power, does mighty works, and gives the community signs.

"We shouldn't get hung up on the miracle, but we should ask what the sign is pointing to," Father Thomas said. "Extraordinary help is for encouragement, or to get your attention, or to let you know that God has something new for you to do. If you get a healing, it's because God wants to put you to work. He didn't heal you to read the funny papers."

Multiplications of food and other supplies have never stopped happening in OLYC's work: Hosts at Mass, sandwiches from plain loaves of bread at one of the jails, pre-wrapped sandwiches at the clinic, money on a trip Father Thomas made to New Zealand, gasoline and a cabinet full of household goods for Sergio and Lucia Conde, sweater sets being distributed to children at the food bank, even highly-specialized bolts for an antenna at KJES after repeated counts had come up four short. Sergio Conde and Francisca Terrazas also report cases in which distant listeners (including Conde himself) have heard tapes being played at KJES when the transmitter wasn't working.

How often does this sort of thing happen? "From time to time," was as close as Father Thomas could come to an estimate. "It's certainly not daily, and it's certainly not weekly." Healings, or reports of healings, are more common: they come up at nearly every Wednesday prayer meeting. Usually nobody bothers to verify them. "If it looks like it's flaky, we don't share it with anybody," Father Thomas said. "If it looks authentic, we share it at the prayer meeting, and if it's really remarkable, we might make it a newsletter."

Here are a few more mighty works testified to by members of the OLYC community:

About 1974, the community established a school at the Juarez dump. But the volunteer teacher had to give up the effort. The students' mental development had been hurt so much by the shortage of protein in their diet that they couldn't even learn their vowels, let alone read or write.

At the time, "healing of memories" was popular in charismatic circles, and some of the women in the community decided to extend the concept to healing intellects. So they laid hands on the youngsters and prayed for exactly that.

A few months later the teacher returned for a visit. Those same unteachable youngsters turned out to greet her, and while she visited they began writing words in the dust on her car. They all went through school afterwards, and one of them became an accountant.

"That's one of our biggest miracles," Father Thomas said.

In 1975, Herminia Montes of El Paso visited the Lord's Ranch because her son was scheduled to receive first Communion there. Montes suffered from severe arthritis. She attended the Mass and the meal of celebration, but when the children and parents went to the swimming pool, she held back. "I was suffering from the soles of my feet to the top of my head," she recalled in a 1999 interview.

So the swimmers in the pool came out and prayed for her, and splashed pool water on her; Father Thomas had blessed the pool, so it was holy water. Then she dipped her own feet into the pool.

"From that day to this…" Montes said, and her voice trailed off as she let her fingers do the talking: grinning broadly, she wiggled them like anybody else, with no pain at all. She stopped taking her medicine soon after she was healed.

In 1991 Montes developed heart trouble, a bad problem in her family. Heart disease had killed her father and some other relatives. She could hardly breathe. Then, on a Saturday retreat at the Lord's Ranch, she decided to pray in front of the Blessed Sacrament. That meant a two-storey climb to the tiny prayer chapel, up a steep staircase. But she made it with no problem breathing, and when she went to her doctor the next week, he couldn't find any problems either.

"Why are you here?" the nurse asked. "Your heart is working like a child's."

The next story is even bigger. In 1978, a group of community members from Juarez were resting at OLYC in El Paso on the way to a charismatic conference at Notre Dame in Indiana. They had had a lot of trouble at the border, and they were tired out, so they were napping on the floor. Father Thomas was asleep on the floor too. Suddenly a nurse who was part of the group found another woman, named Adela, apparently dead—at least, she wasn't showing any vital signs. The nurse woke Father Thomas, who in his grogginess wouldn't agree to call an ambulance ("normally I would have," he said later). He prayed several different ways, including the sacramental anointing of the sick, but nothing helped.

"Finally, I said 'spirit of death, come out in Jesus' name,'" he said. "She got up and started dancing right away, with all the other people." She had been without vital signs for about 10 minutes.[2] Whether Adela was resuscitated from the dead or not, the event was one of a

---

[2] This story was told to me by Father Thomas in a 1999 interview. Father Thomas and Adela herself also testified to the resuscitation at the August 1978 national charismatic conference at Notre Dame, attended by more than 20,000, and the testimony was reported in the November 1978 issue of *New Covenant*.

kind in Father Thomas's experience. "I prayed for another woman to be raised from the dead and she wasn't," he said. "It was a great blow to me." However, two other community members, Tencha Tapia and the late Aurora Villa, have reported relatives returning to life after being apparently dead and, in the case of Tapia's sister-in-law, receiving a death certificate.

Bill Halloran, Mike's father and a community member from 1978 until his death in 2004, told of an incident that took place about 1981. His three-year-old grandson, Robby Delgado, was diagnosed with cancer in one eye, and the eye was scheduled to be removed by surgery. Halloran said he was told in a dream that the surgery should be canceled. When he told the doctor that, there were some hot words, but finally the doctor agreed to have another biopsy done. The cancer was gone.

Bill Halloran also wrote a detailed testimony about his adventures in drilling a well for the Tarahumara Indians of Creel, Mexico, a remote spot about 400 miles from El Paso, in 1990. The Tarahumara had been trying to get a well for 25 years, but every attempt failed because the rock in the area was too hard to drill, so the people had to continue drinking water out of a polluted river. Halloran, who was already 80 at the time, drilled with old equipment for four months, running into problem after problem. Finally, getting near despair, he gave the whole project up to God, and the work speeded up. Soon he hit a rich supply of water, but it turned out to be contaminated with 10 times the safe limit of mercury. He and his wife, Marion, prayed for more than a month, and the next time the water was tested the mercury had dropped to a safe level.

In 1993 Teresa Juarez of El Paso was diagnosed with a brain tumor. The tumor was an aggressive one, expected to spread quickly through her body no matter what treatment she might get. She had headaches and convulsions, she was deaf in her left ear, and she couldn't drive, or even bathe by herself. "The doctor said if I would live three months, that would be a lot," she said in a 1999 interview.

Still, she agreed to a long, brutal program of radiation and chemotherapy. About a third of the way through it, she went to a church across the river in Mexico and prayed to the Virgin Mary. "I said 'go to your Son, as in the wedding of Cana (John 2:1-11), and ask Him to heal me, or His will be done,'" she said. Right away, she felt a pulling sensation on her hair. She could hear out of her left ear, and she felt heat throughout her head and body. She blacked out and had to be carried out of the church; later her friends told her she had cried for two hours. She cancelled the rest of her treatments and went back to her doctor for another brain scan. He agreed only when she signed a release. But the scan found the tumor was gone.

"I haven't had any type of symptom since that moment," she said.

# PART II: SPIRITUAL PRINCIPLES

## CHAPTER 6: DISCERNING GOD'S WILL

From the outside, the OLYC operation is hard to describe in 10 words or less. Is it an evangelistic crusade? A charismatic display of signs and wonders? A social ministry to the poorest of the poor?

In fact, it's all of those things. But as important as they are, they all come in second to something bigger, and at the same time humbler. The point of all OLYC's work is *obedience*. Not to Rick Thomas, the OLYC board, or any human authority, but to God.

"I'm personally trying to be faithful to what God wants me to do, for as long as He has me here," Father Thomas said. "That's what the whole community is doing."

Everything the OLYC community does has something to do with obedience. Take the social ministry—the food banks, the clinics, the services at the old dump site. For most groups involved in work like that, the point would be accomplishment of some sort. But face it: What can 150 people, most of them none too well off themselves, really accomplish for a population of the desperately poor running well up into the hundreds of thousands?

That's the sort of obstacle the OLYC people don't worry about. The things traditional Catholic terminology calls the corporal works of mercy—feeding the hungry, visiting the imprisoned and so on—are matters of obedience, not accomplishment. In Matthew 25, where Jesus compares the last judgment to the separation of the sheep from the goats, those who have done the corporal works of mercy are sent to heaven and those who haven't are sent to hell, "so either you do it, or you're going to have big problems at the general judgment," Father Thomas said. How much OLYC workers actually accomplish is up to God.

It's the same way with evangelism. Preaching comes before service, one way or another, in just about all of OLYC's ministries. That too is obedience: Christ's followers are called on to "make disciples of all nations" (Matthew 28:19).

But these are just generalities. It's normal, more or less, for Christians to feed the hungry and preach the Gospel out of obedience to God. The OLYC people aim at obedience on a much more specific level. They're constantly looking for direction from God to do things like getting locked in jail cells, or taking Christmas dinner to the dump, or buying a new building. This chapter is about how OLYC workers go about getting that direction.

The community looks to many sources for clues to God's will for its ministries. There's prayer, and prophecy, and Church teaching, and the force of circumstances, and even common sense, although "common sense" means something different here than it does to most people. But the key element is a way of reading the Bible that most Christians never try: the way of literal obedience.

"We take God's Word very seriously," Father Thomas said. "Many people would say we're fundamentalists."

In fact, the OLYC people aren't fundamentalists in the usual sense. Fundamentalism, as the word is usually understood, is about taking the Bible literally with respect to the *past*. At OLYC, that's not the point. With his Jesuit education and his shelf full of reference books, Father Thomas knew all about critical Bible scholarship—even obscure points like the influence of ancient Ugaritic (Canaanite) literature on the Psalms—and up to a point he didn't have a problem with it. If some scholars say that the story of Jonah and the large fish wasn't meant to be understood as history, or that St. Paul wasn't the immediate human author of Ephesians, he was open to that.

Instead, the OLYC community takes the Bible literally as a guide to the *present*. The whole Bible is God's Word to us *today*, and our job is to do what it says. If St. Paul didn't in fact write Ephesians, Father Thomas said, "that doesn't affect the contents. I'll leave that to the guys who don't have anything better to do. God gave us the book to tell us what to do, not to argue about what tone of voice He spoke in."

The OLYC community studies the Bible constantly in this spirit of obedience, and it leads to some surprising results. For example, the workers were already giving food to the poor before Christmas 1972, but when they took a closer look they decided that isn't what Luke 14 says. Jesus is talking about holding a banquet, and at a banquet food is not given away; it's *shared* between host and guests. "So we decided to do it," Father Thomas said. "Not approximate it, but *do* it."

And of course, the group learned from that experience that God really *does* multiply food—just like it says in the Bible.

That would be a surprise to a lot of Christians. Nowadays some preachers will tell you that the multiplication of loaves and fishes—the only miracle to find its way into all four Gospels—was nothing more than Jesus challenging the crowd to share the food they'd brought along in their pockets, instead of hoarding it for later.

"If I hadn't had experience to the contrary, I could buy that," Father Thomas chuckled. "But we've seen God do a lot of wonderful things, and we'd have to deny our experience to explain it away."

Of course, taking the Bible literally is not all there is to obeying God. For one thing, there's a warning in the old joke about the man who stuck his finger on a random passage and ended up with Matt. 27:5 ("he [Judas] went and hanged himself"); he tried it again and got Luke 10:37 ("Go and do likewise"). There's also the question of what reading to focus on (why Luke 14 in particular?) and how to apply it in practice (why the dump rather than the beggars on the bridges between El Paso and Juarez?).

Here are some of the clues to God's will that the OLYC community uses along with Scripture reading:

**Common sense:** This one is a bit of a surprise. Most of us would say taking Christmas dinner to a garbage dump runs dead against common sense, but what we really mean is that it's uncomfortable, embarrassing, inconvenient, and just plain weird. "Common sense" in the OLYC definition is based on God's values and priorities, and the dump matched that kind of common sense perfectly: it was the home of people who fit Luke 14 better than anybody else within reach. "God doesn't have any interest in looking good or being respectable," Father Thomas said.

Still, using common sense means the community won't do just any old thing and trust God to take care of it. Some people, Father Thomas said, have suggested that the jail ministry should hand out New Testaments to the inmates. But that isn't going to happen, because common sense says that in that particular jail environment, the Bible pages would end up as toilet paper.

**Circumstances:** To discern God's will, Father Thomas said, look at what's happening around you. Knowing the dump people were there is one example of this, but sometimes circumstances work more powerfully than that. When a new Juarez political administration in the late 1980s shut down the community's juvenile delinquent ministry, the group walked away without a backward glance. "God speaks through circumstances," Father Thomas said. "When He makes something possible He wants you to do it, and when He makes it impossible He wants you to quit."

One of the most important circumstances to look at is human resources: bodies willing to do the work. While the community does not go into debt, it's always ready to step out in faith and trust that God will provide money or other material resources for whatever He appears to want done. "But if you don't have the human resources, it's a sign God doesn't want it done," Father Thomas said. "God can easily supply material resources, but He cannot easily supply human resources because they are dependent on human will and obedience, which He doesn't force."

**Prayer:** Prayer is partly a question of obedience and partly a way of getting the power to do the work (see Chapter 7), but it's also a way of learning God's will—and not merely by asking "God, what should we do?", although that's part of it. It's more a question of keeping the channels of communication open.

"We urge everybody to pray to the max," Father Thomas said. "It keeps you in touch with God, and He can direct you."

"The max" is as much as three hours a day for some people at OLYC. Of course, not everyone there is in a position to do that, but they all pray as much as they can. Father Thomas couldn't give a figure for his own daily prayer because his schedule was so unpredictable; "I try to pray any time I'm not doing something else," he said. The community prays many different ways, including liturgical prayer, spontaneous praise, singing, praying in tongues, the Catholic Liturgy of the Hours, the rosary, and "executing" Scripture (see next chapter). The more the volunteers pray, the clearer sense they tend to have of God's will.

**Prophecy:** The charismatic gift of prophecy, in which an individual delivers a message believed to come from God, can be a big help in discerning God's will. But prophecy isn't usually the main source of an idea for a new project, Father Thomas said, because it isn't usually detailed enough to be used that way. Sometimes prophecy is a confirmation. Sometimes it's a warning or promise.

For example, there was a prophecy in the late eighties that the Lord's Ranch was going to see major changes, but the community didn't take the warning too seriously until circumstances forced the changes. And in 1997, the group was ready to buy a less-than-ideal replacement for the old OLYC building despite Ellen Hogarty's prophecy that God would provide "the perfect place," which this clearly wasn't. So God expressed Himself more forcefully: the community's generous offer for the property was rejected for no apparent reason, and Las Alas—the actual "perfect place"—turned up soon after.

Word of knowledge, a related gift, is more important on a day-to-day level, for example in discovering medical or spiritual problems among those who come to the clinic, so that both prayer teams and doctors can direct their efforts to the problem the Spirit has identified.

**Signs from God:** As mentioned in Chapter 5, apparent miracles are called "signs" in John's Gospel, and they work that way today, too. To Father Thomas, that was the main point of the 1972 Christmas multiplication at the dump. "God was telling us we couldn't abandon those people," he said. "We had to go back."

Another example, from 1979, helped get the jail ministry going. The community had been wrestling with the idea and had decided, with some hesitation, to go ahead. The leaders met at the Lord's Ranch for a weekend retreat to prepare for the ministry, and they held their meetings in a building a few yards from the swimming pool. During the weekend, a well-driller working nearby asked to buy some of the ranch's water. Instead the volunteers let him drain a large amount from the pool for free. That was no problem for the ranch, which has a good water supply. But actually refilling the pool afterwards would have meant running a noisy pump that can be heard half a mile away, and everybody who knew how to run the pump was tied up in the retreat.

"Sunday after lunch we came out and the pool was overflowing with water," recalls Mike Halloran. "That was a clear sign from God." The community decided the jail ministry would be blessed, and went ahead with it.

Around 2001, a long-dry well at Los Jardines de Dios began overflowing just as Father Thomas and Michael Reuter arrived for a visit. It's still working fine today. Father Thomas took that as a confirmation that God will use the land again someday.

**Church authority:** For OLYC as a Catholic organization, one key element in discerning God's will is obedience to the Catholic Church. That means Scripture is never interpreted in a way contrary to Church teachings. It also means orders from bishops and religious superiors are faithfully obeyed. This isn't always an easy matter for a Catholic community that does so many things outside the Catholic mainstream, but God honors this kind of obedience, Father Thomas said.

The Lord's Ranch itself exists only because of obedience to the Church. At one point, the community was offered a square mile of land well east of El Paso, and there was a prophecy that water would be found on it. Father Thomas believed the prophecy and wanted to go ahead and develop the site, but his Jesuit provincial in New Orleans told him to look for something else, so he did. The Lord's Ranch was the result. Meanwhile, water *was* found on the original site, but there wasn't very much of it, and it turned out to be three times as salty as the ocean. No better water has been found there to this day.

**Flexibility:** When OLYC leaders think they know God's will, they keep listening anyway. Whatever way they plan to *do* God's will is probably going to be disrupted by new circumstances. This is also God's guidance.

"Whatever we plan is not God's plan," Father Thomas said. "It's a joke with us, because what we plan early in the morning is changed by the end of the day. We expect it and we just move with it.

"Everybody, including the Church, tends to run on a secular paradigm. But the secret of the spiritual life is docility to the Holy Spirit, whether it's individual or corporate."

"We're trained to think in a certain way," agrees Sergio Conde. "But when you pray, things come out so differently. We pray before we work, we ask for guidance, and we go.

"There isn't too much reasoning. There's faith."

## CHAPTER 7: WORKING IN GOD'S POWER

Some people say faith can move mountains. That expression comes from a couple of well-known Bible passages, but it isn't exactly what the Bible says. And it doesn't really reflect what happens at OLYC, either. What moves mountains is *power*—the power of God.

Faith has been making a comeback in recent years, even in secular circles. Today many psychologists believe that faith can do a lot in people's lives. But the emphasis in popular thought, religious and secular alike, is on the human end. It's the individual's subjective quality of faith—or call it trust, confidence or conviction—that does this work.

There's plenty of trust, confidence and conviction in the OLYC community too, but the work of the ministries isn't done by anything subjective. At OLYC, faith is a *response*, to an objective external reality: God.

The mountain-moving terminology is based mainly on Matt. 17:20, where Jesus says "For truly I tell you, if you have faith the size of a mustard seed, you will say to this mountain, 'Move from here to there,' and it will move; and nothing will be impossible for you." He doesn't say *your faith* will move the mountain, but rather that *you* will.

"God wants us to have power," Father Thomas said. "We are to be victorious with the power of Jesus." Faith is a matter of trusting in that objective power, which comes from outside us, and which we can put to use for God's purposes.

The whole OLYC operation is based on doing very concrete things which the workers have found hook them into the power of God. Three of the most important are prayer, use of Catholic sacramentals[3] such as holy water, and Bible reading in a form called "executing the sentence."

As the last chapter noted, OLYC workers are urged to "pray to the max." Partly, that's a way of staying in touch with God so as to discern His will. But it's also a way of invoking His power.

"We know from experience the more prayer we have, the more clout we have," Father Thomas said. "It's that simple—the more prayer, the more clout. You can see it all the time. Your effectiveness is proportionate to your prayer."

Nothing of consequence is done without prayer in the OLYC community. Workers pray at the start of trips in the car. Father Thomas prayed with me routinely before our many interviews for this book. Volunteers in the

_____

[3] In Catholic teaching, sacramentals, like holy water, are objects or actions approved by the Church for spiritual benefit. They resemble the seven sacraments (baptism, the Eucharist, etc.) in some respects, but are lesser in rank because the sacraments are held to be instituted by Christ Himself and to bestow grace and power in and of themselves.

vans headed for the Juarez ministries pray on the way there; light conversation is kept for the return trip. "Scripture says to pray always, and the ideal is perpetual prayer," Father Thomas said.

At the clinic on the mesa, volunteers follow the four steps of Sir. 38:9-12 in treating patients: the patient should pray, then renounce sin, then use liturgical means (a "sweet-smelling sacrifice" in Sirach, sacramentals and volunteers praying over the patient at the clinic), and *finally*—only as the fourth step—see a doctor.

"Our culture has it all backwards," Father Thomas said. "The [usual] first step is to see a doctor."

OLYC workers use sacramentals—holy water, blessed oil, blessed salt—way beyond ordinary Catholic practice. Father Thomas said official Church prayers over milk jugs full of water, along with other items, on a daily basis. Community members drink holy water and use blessed salt in their food. The lemonade handed out in the jail is made from holy water. If volunteers are worried about hostility in some place they're going, they scatter blessed salt there if they can, in places where it can't be vacuumed up. Even the water in the Lord's Ranch swimming pool has been blessed—not in jugs but right where it stands, in the pool—to make it into holy water.

To a lot of Catholics, let alone Protestants, this all sounds like superstition, and Father Thomas could understand why. "A lot of people tell me 'my priest won't bless it [holy water] because it's superstitious,'" he said.

"I wouldn't believe it myself if I hadn't seen it work. They never told us in seminary that sacramentals work, or spent more than a few minutes on the subject."

But OLYC practice seems to stay clear of the Catholic Church's definition of superstition from the Council of Malines in 1607: "It is superstitious to expect any effect from anything, when such an effect cannot be produced by natural causes, by divine institution, or by the ordination or approval of the Church." Father Thomas said it is always the power of Jesus, never the object itself, that makes sacramentals effective. He said the Bible shows that "God uses material objects to effect spiritual results": Jesus used spittle and mud in healings (John 9:6), and the apostles anointed the sick with oil (Mark 6:13), and used healing cloths (Acts 19:11-12). As for "the ordination or approval of the Church," Father Thomas took literally the wording of the official prayers for blessing sacramentals; the blessing he used for holy water, for example, asks that the water may drive away both disease and demons, and a number of blessings in the Roman Ritual even refer to the drinking of holy water.

What's more, Father Thomas said, when these blessings are said in faith and obedience in the name of Jesus, the power of Jesus enters the sacramentals, and that power will work regardless of whether the recipient believes in it or is even aware of it. Prisoners don't have to know about the blessing to benefit from the holy water lemonade.

"Where the Church acts, Jesus acts," Father Thomas said. "Where the Church blesses, Jesus blesses."

116

Still, he warned, there is some danger of superstition in the use of sacramentals. People should remember that they do not bring "good luck" and that they are no substitute for repentance, or receiving Holy Communion, or Bible study.

"Abuses are always possible, but there's all kinds of abuses in everything," he said. "People go to Communion all the time unworthily. People make marriage vows they have no intention of keeping. But just because the danger is there is no reason not to make use of what God gives us. We need all the help we can get.

"God provides the sacramentals, and the principle is biblically based, both in the Old Testament and the New Testament. You can theorize against it all you want, but they work and they work marvels. We have a file of testimonies from people using sacramentals, because we know people won't believe it."

Father Thomas had plenty of testimonies of his own. One of his favorite stories came from an experience at the Juarez mental hospital around 1990. The volunteers were doing their best to pray for an extremely deranged inmate who had killed his own mother with an axe. It wasn't easy. The man crawled around like a spider and was viciously hostile to the visitors.

"He would say '*vete, vete*' ('go away!'), and he tried to spit on us and pee on us," Father Thomas recalled.

So on each visit the group left behind a jug of holy water. It's hot in Juarez, and there was nothing else convenient, so the man would drink the water. After many visits he calmed down, and over several years he began to act normally and use a wheelchair.

"When he got friendly he would ask us for the '*liquida curativa*,'" Father Thomas said. "He knew it, even though we didn't tell him it was holy water."

The late George Roberts, a retired school custodian from Kansas City who came to the Lord's Ranch annually for years to help with building and repair projects, had a story too. In about 1997, he said, he was trying to clean a drain at La Cueva, an OLYC building used as a residence and for student activities. The building, though dating only from the 1970s, was built in a neighborhood that was once notorious for bootleg liquor operations, and there had been killings in the area. One of the washbasins in the building hadn't drained well for a number of years, and when Roberts tried to clean it out with an industrial auger, the auger seized up and wouldn't go in or come out.

"It just acted like something grabbed it," he said. "It was like it was stuck in concrete."

Roberts hammered away at the job for two hours and got nowhere. Then he tried pouring half a gallon of holy water and half a cup of blessed salt down the drain. Out came 22 feet of auger with no effort, but that wasn't all that came out.

"There was the most awful stench I ever smelled," he said. "My eyes even burned. I ran out of the room."

He clasped a towel over his mouth and nose and went back in to pour more holy water and blessed salt down the drain. Shortly afterward, the stink went away. In its place was "the most beautiful fragrance I ever smelled. I could sell that for perfume. It lasted 20 minutes or half an hour, and the water ran down the drain just like a vacuum cleaner."

Besides prayer and sacramentals, the Bible is also used as a source of God's power. OLYC volunteers not only read the Bible to find out God's will, they read it to *perform* God's will. One example of this is the first visit to the Juarez jail in 1979, where the volunteers read Phil. 2:10-11 until the prisoners' knees *did* bend at the name of Jesus, just like verse 10 says (see Chapter 1). This is sometimes called "executing Scripture." Bible passages are recited over and over to bring about the results they describe. The expression used at OLYC is "executing the sentence," from Ps. 149:9 ("to execute on them the judgment decreed."), and the practice is also based on other scriptural texts: for example, Isa. 55:11, "so shall the word be that goes forth from my mouth; it shall not return to me empty, but it shall accomplish that which I purpose, and succeed in the thing for which I sent it."; Jer. 23:29, in which God's Word is said to be "like fire... like a hammer that breaks a rock in pieces"; and Jer. 1:9-10, where Jeremiah himself is given God's words "to pluck up and to pull down, to destroy and to overthrow, to build and to plant."

"'The word of God is living and active,' (Heb. 4:12), and where it is proclaimed it effects what it says," Father Thomas said. "That's a major biblical principle."

The 1979 jail incident is still the best-known case of successful "execution" by the OLYC community, but there have been many more. Years ago, the community rented a dingy two-room apartment near an El Paso high school and began reading Deut. 28:15-19, curses on disobedience, for two hours a day, with no specific plans beyond that. Students began to drop by out of curiosity, and those who had been involved in the occult would stop with a jolt. "It was like they had been hit with a glove," Father Thomas said. Then they would run outside and vomit. After that they came back in, "ready for Jesus."

Early in 2000, a two-year-old El Paso girl, daughter of a community member, had gone for more than two days whining and crying, sleepy and lethargic. Finally her mother took her next door for prayer, and a neighbor, also a member of the OLYC community, executed Eph. 5:14, "Sleeper, awake! Rise from the dead, and Christ will shine on you." After they had repeated the verse for 20 minutes, Father Thomas said, the girl sat up happily and began to play.

The community has a list of Scriptures to execute in certain circumstances. Psalm 68 ("Let God rise up, let His enemies be scattered;") is often recited in the van on the way to ministries, especially where problems with the occult are suspected. Psalm 52 is also recommended for use against the occult, Eph. 6:18 and 1 Thess. 5:17 at places where prayer has been forbidden (like public schools), and Eph. 5:22-6:4 for family problems. (Warning to male readers: as Father Thomas noted, this last passage lays out duties for *all* family members, so husbands are wrong if they stop with the first verse, "wives, be subject to your husbands.") Readings don't have to be audible to their "targets" to be effective, Father Thomas said.

The principle of executing Scripture also lies behind the KJES radio broadcasts, which are made up entirely of Bible readings except for station identification and a small amount of praise music.

"There's all kinds of garbage in the atmosphere," Father Thomas said. "We're putting out something that's pure. We're putting out the Word of God to take effect in creation."

# CHAPTER 8: ALWAYS THE POOR

One day in the early 1970s, Father Thomas was strolling around the Juarez dump site, chatting with the locals who had turned out for the OLYC ministry. A woman he met invited him to visit her home, so off the two of them went, tramping across mounds of discarded tin cans and other trash to what he figured would be a cardboard shack, or maybe a scrap lumber shanty, perched close to the edge of the dump. But they never got to the edge of the dump.

"We walked across a bunch of cans, and we came to this place, and she said 'this is my home,'" he recalled years later. "There was nothing to show you it was a home. In her mind, this part of the cans was her home."

Poverty. It's literally the first thing anyone with eyes to see will notice about Juarez. Even from the highway along the El Paso side of the Rio Grande, it's easy to look across the narrow river and see the shacks sprawled up and down the low hills on the other side. Turn to your left as you cross any of the three bridges into Mexico, and you'll see the vendors standing in the full glare of the sun, working the long lineups of cars waiting to get back into the States.

Meanwhile, day after day, new poor people from the interior of Mexico stream into Juarez, hoping for $7-a-day jobs in the local *maquiladoras* (border zone factories) or a chance to get across the river into a wealthier land. It's the new people who spread out on the edges of Juarez, building whole new neighborhoods where concrete block homes count as upper middle class and adobe is lower middle. Scrap wood, cardboard (a refrigerator box makes a convenient outhouse), corrugated metal and tar paper (held down with bricks or fist-sized rocks to make a roof) are other popular building materials. And all the people in the ramshackle houses have to survive on what little they can earn, beg or steal, because there's no U.S.-style welfare system in Mexico.

It's no surprise that a ministry like OLYC would concern itself so heavily with poverty, not when close to a million desperately poor people are almost literally scrabbling at a chain link fence a few blocks away. But Father Thomas has been looking for the poor since long before he came to El Paso, and finding them wherever he goes. When Jesus said "You always have the poor with you" (John 12:8), He wasn't kidding.

"There are poor everywhere," Father Thomas said. In the early 50s, before his ordination, he taught high school in Dallas, and he used to take his students to visit the slums, much to the distress of their parents and his own fellow-teachers. He did the same thing in New Orleans as a newly-ordained priest. Racial

124

segregation was the big issue at the time; on one occasion in New Orleans he took the teenagers to a racetrack, where they shot photos in the stables where the thoroughbred horses lived, and then to a black neighborhood, where they took pictures of the housing the poor lived in. "They saw the horses were treated better than the people," he said. Evy Nelson remembers him growing food for the poor in his back yard in El Paso in the 60s, and throughout his life, when he traveled on speaking engagements, he sought out the poor—even in places where his hosts claimed there was no poverty.

Why all this emphasis on the poor? First of all, like everything else at OLYC, it's a matter of obeying God. "Helping the poor is all over Scripture," he said. "It's not just in Matthew 25. It's in Job, and the Psalms, and Deuteronomy, and Proverbs. And it's in Church history, too. The greatest heroes of the Church are martyrs, and a few outstanding intellectuals, and the rest are all helpers of the poor."

Another reason is simple justice, Kingdom-style. "God hears the cry of the poor," Father Thomas said. "Justice would demand that I don't live like Superhog when my brother is starving to death. We're all in the family of God. There has to be sharing, not gross inequality."

Poverty, actually, is a consequence of sin—of the fact that too many people, rich and poor alike, have chosen the wrong side in the ongoing battle between the Kingdom of God and the kingdom of Satan (see Chapter 10). And our reaction to poverty is one way to tell the difference between those kingdoms.

125

"Jesus says give, the devil says grab," Father Thomas preached at every opportunity. For example, see Luke 3:11, "Whoever has two coats must share with anyone who has none; and whoever has food must do likewise." "If we took that seriously, there would be no economic difference between El Paso and Juarez," he said.

Still another reason for a focus on poverty is the spiritual benefit that comes from making genuine contact with the poor. "As soon as you do that, you're going to have a conversion, unless you're extremely hard-hearted," Father Thomas said. "You'll see they're the same as you."

Finally, there's Jesus' own example. He was born into poor circumstances—the two turtle doves sacrificed by Joseph and Mary at Jesus' presentation in the temple (Luke 2:24) were the offering prescribed for those too poor to give larger animals, Father Thomas noted. In His adult life, Jesus had "nowhere to lay His head." (Matthew 8:20) "He slept outdoors a lot," Father Thomas said. Then He was buried in a borrowed grave. "If you're going to be like Christ, He shows us how."

When it comes to working with the poor, Father Thomas said, an awful lot of showing how is needed, for Church workers and secular workers alike. For many people, especially in churches, "helping the poor" means giving a donation that ends up doing more for the giver in terms of personal satisfaction than it does for the recipient in terms of help. Christmas is a bad time for this sort of thing—people want to give turkeys to slum dwellers who don't have ovens to cook them, or toys to children who don't have enough to eat; and even if the donors give useable food to the hungry at Christmas, that does nothing to solve the year-around need. "We have a lot of problems with that," Father Thomas said. "They [donors] have this good feeling, and that's what they want, but it doesn't really help the poor."

Government and secular agencies have another problem: they can't deal with the spiritual aspect of poverty. One of the biggest problems of the poor is sin, Father Thomas said, and the remedy for it is repentance and the grace of God, which government as an institution obviously can't offer. It isn't that the poor are any more sinful than the rich or the middle class, but the consequences of sin in this world tend to be worse for the poor. If a breadwinner loses a job for drinking or stealing, there's usually nobody to take up the slack. If a wife is deserted by her husband, or has reason to leave him because of adultery or abuse, her chances of finding a decent job to support herself are just about zero. If a family member gets a venereal disease or needs help with substance abuse, the family probably won't be able to afford treatment, especially in Mexico.

At the same time, there are some spiritual pluses in poverty, and Christians who work with the poor need to keep them in mind—for their own sake as well as for the sake of the poor. "God tries some people with possessions and some with want of possessions," Father Thomas said. "Those who have a want of possessions seem to pass the test better. The poorer a person is, the more ready he is to share, and the richer a person is, the less willing he is to share. The women at the food bank save money to give to the Church and the needy, and to share for each other's needs. Aurora Villa (a longtime community leader from Juarez who died in 2007) [took] whole families into her home for three months at a time. Not many middle-class people would do that."

What makes the poor so much more open? Father Thomas cited the parable of the sower (Mark 4:1-20), and especially the thorns of worldly concerns (verses 7 and 18-19) that choke off the seed of God's Word. "The poor have been stripped of thorns. When the Word is planted it can produce. Rich people have been cultivating thorns for years. They don't need to turn to God—they have money in the bank and all that. But the poor don't have any other resources. God is their only hope."

Deciding how to help the poor is never easy. It's harder yet in a place like Juarez, where the numbers are so huge, the poverty so desperate, and the social service net so limited, where witchcraft, wife abuse and male adultery are considered normal. It's in the face of this challenge that the OLYC workers remember that their work is a matter of obedience, not accomplishment.

"I used to really concern myself about that," Father Thomas said. "Where do you begin in such a sea of misery? My view now is that you do what you can with the resources you have. God indicates what He wants you to do by the resources He gives you.

"We are not divine providence. We do what we can."

In an American or Canadian city, where the poverty is less desperate and the social service net is much better, the basic approach is the same but the challenge is a little different. Father Thomas didn't see government assistance as the perfect solution to poverty, but he didn't sneer at it either. Government programs can meet some needs, and that leaves fewer needs for Christian groups to worry about. On the other hand, the poor can be harder to find (in some communities they all live in certain neighborhoods, in others they're spread through the general population, in still others they're homeless), and it's crucial to find out what is or is not being done to help them. To do that, you need to turn to somebody other than the government.

"Find out who in this city helps the poor out of *agape* (supernatural) love and not because they're being paid," Father Thomas said. "That person would tell you what's being done and what's not being done."

And of course, whether in Mexico or in the States, prayer is essential for getting God's guidance, in work with the poor or in any other ministry.

Here are a few other principles followed in OLYC's work among the poor:

**Changing unjust structures and meeting immediate needs are *both* important.** OLYC doesn't shy away from political activism. In 1966, when the Texas poll tax that had kept many Mexican farm workers off the voters' list was declared unconstitutional, OLYC people dived in to help during a two-week voter registration period that saw about 20,000 people sign up. Father Thomas handed out registration forms outside factories and another volunteer hand-delivered the completed forms to the local courthouse despite a rule that they were supposed to be mailed in individually. "It was all over the newspapers," Father Thomas said. "Where did all these forms come from?" A very different chance at political work came during Sergio Conde's three years in Juarez municipal government.

But opportunities for this sort of thing are limited. Opportunities for meeting the day-to-day needs of the poor are unlimited, just like Jesus said. "You have to be aware of unjust structures and work on them," Father Thomas said, "but changing them can't be done in a moment. It takes years and years, and you have to do it when the Lord makes it possible. If you don't meet the immediate needs, a lot of people are suffering in the meantime."

**Show people their own riches.** The poor may not have money, but they have many talents and gifts that can be used to help themselves, and better still, other people. They can pray; they can sing; they can smile; they can babysit or clean houses or wash clothes for one another. They can work together. "Everybody is gifted by God," Father Thomas said, "but poor people are so beaten down they don't know they have those gifts." He liked to point out Ephesians 1:3-5 to them: "I tell them before God made the sun, He chose you. They say, 'you mean I'm not a trash bag?'"

**Teach them to give rather than grab.** Giving is the rule in God's Kingdom, and grabbing is the rule in the other place. This applies even to the poor. At the food bank, there's a box labeled "it is more blessed to give than to receive," to hold donations of food from people who are themselves recipients of food. The poor respond well to this, Father Thomas said: some even offered him money to help him pay his bridge toll back into El Paso. "Everybody has something they can give," Father Thomas said. "If they can't work, they can pray."

A rule like this one can't be applied mechanically. OLYC volunteers don't give handouts indiscriminately, and they avoid giving to professional beggars, who might be just as successful at what they do as anybody in any other trade. On the other hand, need is need, and they don't turn away from it just to make a point. "We give a lot of things away with no strings attached," Father Thomas said, "but we're always working toward getting the poor to give as well as receive."

This policy has worldly as well as spiritual benefits, Father Thomas said, in that it helps teach people not to be dependent and moves them toward self-sufficiency. But he says it's hard to measure success in this area, for OLYC as well as for secular agencies. "No one is ever truly self-sufficient," he said.

**Manage your own material goods appropriately.** If you care about the poor, you should live simply yourself. But that doesn't mean you need to become desperately poor. "God wants everybody to live in decency and comfort appropriate to human beings," Father Thomas said. "Because of the maldistribution of wealth, this is not occurring. We try to make the distribution more just. But we cannot serve the poor if we are as handicapped as they are."

OLYC volunteers are careful to avoid unnecessary expenditure, but the community will spend whatever is necessary to do its work. Its vehicles, for example, are spartan, but kept in top running condition.

**Deal with sin.** The OLYC ministries put a high priority on meeting material needs, but not in isolation from spiritual needs. In working with the poor, and in every other work, they preach repentance from sin— witchcraft, substance abuse, family violence, adultery and many other practices.

Along with promoting responsibility, self-help and giving rather than grabbing, the battle against sin is part of the war against a way of life that keeps people poor. Sin is one more link in the chain of poverty, and people who break that link will be better off, even in secular terms.

But preaching repentance is also part of evangelism, which is a top priority for OLYC. And there's more at stake in evangelism than breaking one link in the chain of poverty.

## CHAPTER 9: GO AND MAKE DISCIPLES

How many people in the world need to be evangelized? Almost seven billion, and growing every day.

The market for evangelism—the preaching of the Gospel—includes the prisoners in the Juarez jail, and the crowd at the OLYC prayer meetings, and all those people who go to Billy Graham crusades. But it also includes Billy Graham himself. And the Pope, too. Not to mention Rick Thomas, during his lifetime, and the whole gang at OLYC, even the most dedicated. Everybody needs to be evangelized, not just once but continually.

Evangelism, as the OLYC people see it, is preaching repentance and drawing people closer to God. Sometimes it starts at a very low level, if people have never heard of Jesus, or if they turned their backs on Him a long time ago. Sometimes it starts at a much higher level. But there's no such thing as the level where it stops.

"The needs are more severe in some people than others," Father Thomas said, "but the process is still the same. People may not be into big-time sin. Their sin may be that they haven't discerned God's will for them and embraced it in a complete way.

"We do that with ourselves, too. We examine our consciences and say 'what did I do today, what was sinful, what was less perfect or less generous?' The Pope himself goes to confession regularly. What does he confess? I don't know—he's not a heroin addict. He would be going through repentance and coming closer to God."

Evangelism OLYC-style, you may have noticed by now, goes way beyond "soul-winning," in either a Catholic or an evangelical Protestant sense. "We don't use the term 'soul-winning,'" Father Thomas said. "A lot of people want to get people 'saved,' and by that they mean the Sinner's Prayer. I don't think that's theologically sound. You're justified in this life, but you're not saved until you're in heaven. If you count up all the people who are 'saved' in this country you'd have a bunch, but you look around and see the mess we're in. 'Salvation' has very little effect for most of them.

"We see evangelism as a much deeper and longer process than simply getting people to parrot the Sinner's Prayer. If people don't become disciples, then we've failed."

Father Thomas didn't condemn Billy Graham-style evangelism. In fact, he volunteered as a Catholic counselor with the traveling Protestant evangelist Luis Palau's crusades in El Paso. But he did have some reservations about that approach. He agreed with the traveling preachers that what is at stake in evangelism is people's eternal destiny—heaven or hell, in other words. What he disagreed with is any suggestion, intentional or otherwise, that answering a crusade altar call is all it takes to get into heaven.

So what *does* it take? Who *does* go to heaven? Every evangelical who has accepted Jesus as Lord and Savior? Every Catholic who goes to Mass on Sunday and stays clear of mortal sin? Father Thomas wouldn't answer that question directly—"I would just be giving an opinion"—but what he did have to say won't be reassuring to anybody who might be hoping to scrape by on the Catholic or Protestant minimum.

It's true that the Bible says Jesus died for everybody (2 Cor. 5:14-15) and that God wants everybody to be saved (1 Tim. 2:4). But whether it will work out that way is another question. Jesus Himself was once asked if only a few will be saved, and He responded with some tough advice: "Strive to enter through the narrow door; for many, I tell you, will try to enter and will not be able." (Luke 13:24). "That's as close as the New Testament comes to answering the question," Father Thomas said. "Jesus doesn't answer it. He doesn't say yes, He doesn't say no, He doesn't say 10 per cent."

But at the same time, Father Thomas noted that the word "strive" in the verse from Luke is the Greek *agonizomai*, "struggle," the origin of the English word "agony." And that's why the OLYC people believe evangelism is a lifelong process: it's never safe to stop the struggle.

"We're taking Jesus' advice seriously," Father Thomas said. "I would say it would be disobedient and risky not to take that advice. Jesus is the best witness about the

135

next life, and if other people aren't echoing what Jesus said, they're just giving an opinion that has no basis in Scripture."

To an evangelical, this talk about struggle might sound like salvation by works, but in fact neither the Catholic Church nor Father Thomas is saying salvation can be earned; for Catholics as for Protestants, salvation is a gift from God which no one can earn. "You're justified by faith in Jesus Christ, but faith has to take what Jesus said and act on it," he said. "If it doesn't, it's dead." And as for the Catholic who feels safe because he hasn't committed any mortal sins lately, "what's he doing about sins of omission? The Confiteor (the prayer of sorrow for sin, recited at every Mass) also says '…what I failed to do.'"

As to the usual questions about hell, Father Thomas didn't claim to have inside information. He wasn't sure whether it's a place of actual physical fire, and he wasn't prepared to say that all non-Christians—from your atheist cousin to tribes that have never heard of Jesus— are going to go there. Only God knows those things; God is merciful and He wants everybody to be saved. Nevertheless, hell is real, it's a real possibility for everyone, and it's terrible; the images of fire and worms in the Bible may or may not be literal, but they aren't there to be ignored. "Hell is separation from God," Father Thomas said. "We're made for God, so hell is eternal deprivation of what we're made for.

"I think you need to do a lot to keep other people out of hell. That's just the outworking of *agape* love. That's a very valid motive. If you don't care if he goes to hell, you don't have much love for your neighbor. If that's the only way you can get a guy to move, by putting a torch to him, that's better than not moving at all. Jesus talks a lot about hell, and He uses it as motivation, so it's not to be despised."

Anyhow, Father Thomas said, we don't need to know all the answers. We aren't in charge of people's eternal destination—God is. We *are* in charge of spreading the word. "We are commanded to 'proclaim the good news to the whole creation'" (Mark 16:15), Father Thomas said. "That's our job."

Evangelism isn't usually free-standing at OLYC. It's closely tied in with the community's other ministries. Father Thomas didn't agree with people who say only spiritual needs are important, but he didn't agree with people who say you have to meet material needs before you can preach the Gospel, either. OLYC workers do *both*, in whatever proportions fit the circumstances.

"Ideally they go together," Father Thomas said. "But that doesn't always work. Sometimes people aren't open to hearing the Gospel, but they're in need, and you still help them if you can. Or at the jail, we usually preach first and hand out the food afterward, but if some guys come late [brought back to the cell by the guards], we feed them anyway. I don't think we even reflect on which is more important."

In one sense all OLYC workers—and all good Christians—are evangelizing all the time, because everything done for the Kingdom counts, whether it's preaching, feeding the hungry, saying prayers, living the simple life, or being kind to people you meet. "Evangelism occurs whenever one does God's will," Father Thomas said. "You don't have to be saying a word." For example, 1 Pet. 3:1 speaks of how unbelieving husbands "may be won over without a word by their [Christian] wives' conduct"; "The wife evangelizes the husband without saying a word," Father Thomas said.

On the other hand, OLYC workers definitely preach the Gospel in words, too. Evangelism by preaching is part of most of the ministries—in the jails, at the clinic, in the mental hospital, at the food bank, at the prayer meetings at Las Alas, to visitors at the Lord's Ranch. Once in a while the workers do street evangelism in Juarez or El Paso; this usually happens if there are visitors who are interested in learning how. And virtually always, when OLYC people are invited out of town, they end up teaching their hosts how to evangelize; they have done this in Canada, in Trinidad, in England and in a number of other countries.

What, exactly, they say depends to some degree on circumstances—who they're talking to, how much time they have, and so on. But the variations are always a matter of hanging different amounts of "flesh" on what they call the "bare bones" of the Gospel, the standard Christian account of the events of salvation:

God made everything, they say, and everything obeys God—except people. God didn't want to send people to hell for disobedience, so God the Father sent God the Son to offer forgiveness of sins and eternal life. He took flesh by the Virgin Mary and grew up as a normal human being, except He didn't sin. He was crucified, died, was raised from the dead, and now reigns in heaven; He offers pardon and eternal life to those who turn to Him and turn away from sin. "So," the talk usually ends, "would *you* like to do that?"

Apart from the content, they try hard to follow a few other rules:

**Have prayer support.** On those street evangelism expeditions, 90 per cent of the group will be praying while 10 per cent are talking to people.

**Be personally authentic**, in your lifestyle and behavior as well as your message. "We have to *be* the good news and not just talk *about* the Good News," Father Thomas said. "If we talk about the Good News and are personally the bad news, it's not going to be very effective."

**Suit your message to your hearer.** St. Paul himself talked one way to Jews and another to Greeks (compare his sermon in the synagogue of Antioch in Pisidia, Acts 13:16-43, with his speech in the public square in Athens, Acts 17:22-24). Do your best to say "whatever that person would accept without turning them off," Father Thomas said. God's revelation has always been gradual—the moral teaching in the Old Testament is laxer than what's in the New Testament, for example— and people can only take so much at a time,

**Don't forget repentance.** Suiting the message to your hearer does *not* mean you should be afraid to confront the issue of personal sin, but there are no blanket rules as to how or when. "Repentance is part of

139

the package, and you bring it up when you're able to," Father Thomas said. "You've got to use common sense." One factor to keep in mind is an order of priority. A man who beats his wife has to stop that first, and then he can work on not stealing tools from his job, and then on lesser sins. "The Holy Spirit convicts of sins gradually," Father Thomas said. "People can't deal with all their sins at one time." Still, they're going to have to start dealing with them, and evangelism includes telling them that.

"Repentance is left out nowadays because it's unpopular," Father Thomas said. "But it's an essential part of the Gospel. You come to God as you are, but you don't stay as you are. God wants us to make changes. The way God loves you, He wants to start scrubbing you up. It's not toleration. If there's no repentance, there's no serious coming to God."

# CHAPTER 10: A TALE OF TWO KINGDOMS

At OLYC, spiritual realities are matters of everyday experience. The power of God and the joy of the Holy Spirit have gotten to be just as concrete and obvious as the sidewalk underfoot, and just as impossible to imagine away. It's a lot like living next door to heaven.

Unfortunately, that isn't the whole story. As anyone there will tell you, there are two kinds of spiritual realities. Because of its work, the community also lives close enough to hell to hear the crackling of the flames. And nobody ever forgets it—or lets visitors forget it.

"Our battle is not against people but against the spiritual forces working in and around these people" (based on Eph. 6:12), state the community guidelines at the Lord's Ranch. What's more, the world of darkness has a lot of advantages in the short run.

"There's lots of visible kingdoms in the world, but there's only two invisible kingdoms," Father Thomas preached on a regular basis. "There's the kingdom of God, and the kingdom of Satan. And most people are experiencing the kingdom of Satan most of the time."

The devil's kingdom shows up everywhere, Father Thomas said. It shows up in sin, in worry, in sickness, in greed, in negative attitudes. It shows up in ordinary Anglo-Saxon superstitions and in most popular music, rock and otherwise. In El Paso, and especially in Juarez, it shows up in the almost subhuman poverty, in the brutality both of criminals and of some government officials, and in occult practice at a level the average Anglo can hardly even imagine. And fighting that world of darkness—spiritual warfare, it's called—is the point of the entire OLYC operation.

"Spiritual warfare is part and parcel of evangelization and ministry," Father Thomas said. "It was with Jesus, and it is with us. The only difference is that He was better at it."

Newcomers generally get their first taste of this warfare over some innocent-sounding remark. Visitors used to joke about this—"don't say 'good luck,' Father Thomas is listening"—but the OLYC gang isn't joking. Anything to do with superstition, even a routine expression like "good luck" that most people don't mean in a superstitious way, is regarded as part of the kingdom of Satan. But the battle isn't just fought over superstition or occult practices. *All* the OLYC ministries are about spiritual warfare. Whatever is good for God and His children is bad for Satan, and vice-versa.

Take the jail ministry. Volunteers start each visit by praying Pope Leo XIII's prayer against the devil, and they execute anti-Satan Scriptures outside the cells. They serve the prisoners lemonade made from holy water. They preach the Gospel, and call the prisoners to repentance. They also feed them fruit and sandwiches, and over the years they have influenced the guards directly and indirectly to stop the torture of prisoners, which was standard operating procedure before the ministry started. At the food bank there's more prayer, preaching and Scripture; people also get food and medical treatment. And all of it counts as spiritual warfare, because all of it advances the Kingdom of God.

"The kingdom of Satan suffers a loss at every point," Father Thomas said.

The community's most spectacular teaching on spiritual warfare concerns the occult. It starts with the first commandment (Exod. 20: 2-6) [4], which begins "I am the Lord your God...you shall have no other gods before me." The first commandment tends to be the forgotten commandment, Father Thomas said, so much so that his seminary courses spent less time on the first commandment than they did, for example, on the morality of an obscure sexual practice he never again heard of after ordination. But in fact the first commandment is the most important of all, the only one that specifies that God is actually jealous over it (verse 5). "When we break this commandment, we are opening the door and kissing the devil," Father Thomas said. "That's why God is jealous."

And the devil can be very stubborn about breaking off that kiss. This is the story of a community member I'm going to call "Lupe," though that isn't her real name.

---

[4] While the content of the 10 Commandments is the same for both Catholics and Protestants, the two groups traditionally number them differently. For Catholics, the first commandment runs through verse 6 and includes the prohibition on idolatry.

Lupe was born in Mexico but moved across the border to the El Paso area as a child. She was raised in an abusive environment and she had a troubled marriage, including a 10-year adulterous affair. Over the course of her life she has been exposed to witchcraft from many directions. Ancestors on both sides of her family practiced it, and so did her husband's family. One of her friends put a spell on Lupe's boyfriend. An enemy she made in a tenancy dispute put a spell on Lupe herself. Even a priest she consulted sent her to an occult practitioner.

Over the years she has suffered from a long list of illnesses. These include severe chronic shoulder pains, psychological collapse, and the one she noticed most, a burning sensation which was at its worst during intercourse, "like I had hot jalapeños [fiery Mexican peppers] in me." She tried medical treatment and psychiatry, but none of it did her any good. Then she felt a revelation from the Virgin Mary to go see Father Thomas, a man she had never met.

Father Thomas told her to read Psalms 68 and 91 regularly, to pray for her ancestors, and to use sacramentals, for herself, her husband, and her home.

"After two weeks I got up [psychologically] like that," she says, snapping her fingers. Her physical problems took longer to go away, and they still come back when she meets people with evil spirits.

"It's weird, but it's reality, and I'm living in it," she says. "Once you do this [Father Thomas's instructions],

Jesus starts forgiving your sins and He starts putting everything back together."

None of this was any surprise to Father Thomas. He couldn't explain Lupe's experiences, but he didn't doubt them either. When it comes to evil spirits, he said, "I know enough to know I don't know much. A lot of people know what they do and how to discern them, but what they *are*, not much is known about that."

What do evil spirits do? According to Father Thomas, they're the reason fortune tellers really do provide accurate information sometimes, and spiritualists or Mexican *curanderas* (folk healers) really do cure illnesses.

"Spiritualists truly heal, but they heal by a forbidden power," he said. "Not every spiritual healing is a healing from God." Even charismatic gifts such as tongues and prophecy can be counterfeited by the devil.

It's against this background that Father Thomas took his strong stand against anything near the occult, including not only "good luck" but horoscope reading ("a very ancient form of devil worship"), fortune telling, and a long list of other ordinary things, right down to wishing on a star or on birthday candles. He would not perform a wedding unless the bride and groom agreed not to let their guests throw rice, a custom with a pagan background.

"I recognize that I'm extreme," he said. "But I'm dealing with people who are up to *here* in occult practices. The devil has his sacramental system just like

God does—he just imitates what God does—and you've got to be careful which system you're involved with."

How can we find our way through all of this? Here's the basic principle. Father Thomas said everything worth having—information, gifts, power, protection—comes from one of three sources: from God, from the natural world (thus also ultimately from God) or from the devil. Getting these things from the first two sources is acceptable, as long as what we're doing isn't sinful in some other way. It is OK for a sick person to ask God for healing; it is also OK to go to the doctor. It is not OK to undergo a limpia ("cleansing") by a *curandera* when it's based on spiritual techniques "outside the lordship of Jesus Christ." No practices of a spiritual nature are permitted if they are not within the framework of the Bible or the Church.

Not only practices but objects—"the devil's sacramentals"—are a problem. These include idols, such as statues of Buddha, and good luck charms, like rabbit's feet. Father Thomas remembered a healing service where a woman who was blind in one eye asked him to pray for her. She was wearing a Zodiac (astrological sign) ring, and he refused to pray for her until she took it off.

"She said 'I can't get rid of it.' I said 'I won't pray, then.' We went back and forth for a while. Finally she took it off and handed it to me. I put it on the cement floor and smashed it with my heel. She got her sight back immediately."

Father Thomas didn't, in fact, throw out everything that somebody might think is occult. He wouldn't, for example, get rid of a book on comparative religion just because it had pictures of idols. OLYC workers handle money like everybody else, even though American banknotes have Masonic symbols and Mexican money has images of pagan gods.

The key factor with any physical object is the intention of its maker—whether occult influence has been invited into it. If so, the object should be smashed, burned, or even melted (see Deut. 12:3); it should never be thrown away for someone else to pick up.

All occult objects and practices open the door to Satan, Father Thomas said, and once Satan gets inside, he'll stay inside, for generations, even, until he is chased out. The fact that people don't know they are violating the first commandment, or don't really believe in the superstition they practice—for example, when people visit a fortune teller for fun—makes no difference in this respect.

"I meet people every week who are sick because they violated the first commandment, and their cure depends on their repentance," Father Thomas said. "I don't think all illness is caused by Satan, but I think there's a frequent connection between sin and illness—not necessarily personal sin, but social sin or ancestral sin."

He called on everyone to repent and renounce formally, out loud, all sins against the first commandment and all involvement with the occult, whether knowing or not, from Ouija boards and water witching to knocking on wood or crossing fingers for luck; then acknowledge the lordship of Jesus, ask Him to cleanse us from the occult, and command occult spirits in Jesus' name to go away from us and stay away (see prayer at end of chapter). We should do the same for any such sins by our ancestors.

A special warning for Catholics concerns the danger of idolatry in dealing with statues, crucifixes and other images used by the Church. Christian images are good in themselves, Father Thomas said; the Church has approved them from an early date, and they are supposed to remind us of Jesus or the saints the way a wallet photo reminds us of our sweetheart or our child. But attributing power to a statue itself, or worshipping it, is idolatry.

Another difficult case is dealing with non-Christian religions. They can't simply be treated as part of the kingdom of Satan, Father Thomas said. Some of their beliefs are true, and some of their practices might be harmless or even beneficial in themselves. The Second Vatican Council said the Church "rejects nothing of what is true or holy in these religions" (*Nostra Aetate*, Section 2). But Father Thomas said this statement has been blown out of proportion by a lot of Catholics, and has been turned into an excuse for accepting elements of other faiths that are neither true nor holy. Non-Christian religions contain false beliefs as well as true ones, and any practice or ritual that hasn't been or can't be separated from the false beliefs is off limits for Christians. "Discernment has to be used in this area, and in my experience, most people don't have the discernment," Father Thomas said. When in doubt, non-Christian religions should be left alone.

Anyhow, there's more to resisting Satan's kingdom than just steering clear of false worship or occult activities. The battle between the two kingdoms cuts right across every area of life, and in every case it's a Christian's duty to avoid Satan's influence.

To take another example that gets a lot of attention from visitors to the community, Father Thomas talked about popular music much the same way he talked about "good luck." Music, like everything else, comes from one of three sources, he said. Some of it is inspired by the Holy Spirit, and some of it is human and innocent. But he said the majority of the music on the radio is from the devil—not because it necessarily has Satanic lyrics or occult intentions, but because it serves the devil's purposes. If it keeps you from praying easily—and this would cover most loud, jarring or even up-tempo music—it's doing the devil's work in you; the same is true if it tempts you to bad or sinful thoughts, which would cover not only rock lyrics but much of today's country music and many other categories. ("Country is worse than rock because you can understand the words," laughs Michael Reuter, the ex-heavy metal fan.) Still, the community's strongest opposition is to rock, which the volunteers see as the most destructive overall.

The list goes on. Innocent worldly concerns can do the devil's work if we think about them the wrong way. Worry, anxiety, a negative outlook—all of that comes from the devil, Father Thomas said, because the Bible tells us not to worry.

"Jesus' promise is that His yoke is easy and His burden is light" (Matt. 11:30), Father Thomas said, "so if our yoke is not easy and our burden is not light, we'd better check to see whose yoke we're carrying.

"God tells us our thoughts should be on whatever is true, honest, pure, admirable, decent and worthy of respect [paraphrasing Phil. 4:8]. People have a lot of psychological problems because they spend so much time thinking about things that aren't true, honest, pure, admirable, decent or worthy of respect."

Father Thomas didn't oppose psychology any more than he opposed medicine—"it's a good and necessary science"—and he didn't suggest all psychological problems can be cured by religious means. But he did say secular psychological practice suffers from a lack of awareness of sin and the role it plays in mental problems by exposing us to the devil's influence.

Still, the one area that's most caught up in the devil's kingdom, even (or especially) among Christians, isn't superstition or rock music or negative thoughts. The pagan gods or Masonic symbols on the money circulating around El Paso and Juarez aren't doing half the spiritual harm the money itself, or people's attitude toward it, is doing. We can stay away from good luck charms and turn off the radio, but we all use money, and all of us have absorbed Satan's message about money to some degree. We all accept without question that making money is extremely important. For a lot of people, though hopefully not for most Christians, money is the chief goal of life; and even for the rest of us, Christians included, it's a high priority, if only to pay the bills.

God's message is different, Father Thomas said. "You have received without payment; give without payment." And that covers everything, including whatever goods or services we're selling now to make a living. "A hundred years ago you had nothing, you were nothing. Everything you have is received without payment." That's why the OLYC community doesn't fundraise, why it gives its services and its tapes and sacramentals away, why it urges members to work for the Lord without pay and trust Him for their needs.

"When it comes to money, Jesus says give, the devil says grab," Father Thomas said. "That's the easiest way to tell the two kingdoms apart. If you want to inhibit the spread of the kingdom of God, introduce the love of money."

And that, Father Thomas said, is where the devil is still doing his most effective work. Even in the OLYC community.

First, remember all the sins against the first commandment that you can recall committing, whether deliberately or accidentally, whether believing in what you were doing or not. Then pray as follows:

"God, I confess all these sins against the first commandment – sins of superstition, idolatry and witchcraft. I repent. I ask Your forgiveness. I'm very sorry for having offended You. I turn from all these sins.

"Jesus, I take You as my Savior, my only Lord. I ask You to wash me clean in Your precious blood—wash my mind, wash my heart, wash my soul, wash my body. I love You, Jesus.

"I also want to confess all the sins against the first commandment that my parents, my grandparents, and all my ancestors committed. I confess them now and turn from them. I ask Your forgiveness for these sins. Take them away, Lord Jesus. You are my Savior.

"All occult spirits I command you to go away in the name of Jesus Christ. I close the door on all occult spirits forever. I open myself up completely to the Holy Spirit. I take Jesus as my Lord and Savior. Thank You, Jesus. I love You, Jesus. Praise be to You Lord Jesus Christ, now and forever."

## CHAPTER 11: THE ONE THING LACKING

Now that you've read this far, is there anything bothering you?

I think there should be. Anyhow, there's something bothering me. It has been for years. It bothered Father Thomas, too.

If what OLYC is doing is so great, why isn't it a whole lot greater?

If that sounds like a strange question, let me explain it by putting myself into the story in a way I have been trying to avoid up to now.

It has been more than 20 years since I first visited OLYC. I've read the articles, heard the stories, met most of the main people, tagged along on most of the ministries. I've never been present for a miracle, but I've seen more than enough to convince me that the "mighty works" of God in the OLYC ministries are real.

I guess the experience that did the most to convince me was my first visit to the Juarez jail, in 1989. I was locked in a cell with three or four other volunteers, the way I've described, and one of them was preaching to 20 or 30 inmates. They were all listening, but that in itself doesn't prove much. Anything is more interesting than staring at a concrete floor.

Then a guard showed up at the door with an order of cigarettes. The inmates in this cell had sent out for cigarettes—you can do that in a Mexican jail, if you have the money—and the cigarettes had arrived. Ignoring the sermon, the prisoners stampeded for the door and grabbed their cartons. The preacher, a middle-aged, baseball-cap-wearing man from Juarez named Gabriel, waited until they had come back to their places with their cartons in hand. Then he asked them not to smoke.

"This is God's time," he told them in good-humored Spanish. "You can smoke later."

Right, I thought. Who's going to stop 20 jailbirds in the middle of a nicotine fit? Gabriel has reached a bit too far this time.

But the prisoners all nodded cheerfully. Nobody lit up. The sermon went ahead, and most of the inmates were on their knees for the prayer at the end.

OK, strictly speaking that story doesn't prove anything either. It just happens to be my favorite. But there are dozens of other stories like that, my own and other people's, and some of them are a lot bigger.

I've seen destitute people from the slums of west Juarez turn out before sunrise on a bitterly cold February morning to dance and praise God on the food bank mesa. I've talked to two people who were there at the Christmas multiplication of 1972, and four who were in the Juarez jail for the first OLYC visit in 1979. I've heard ordinary, everyday people tell about being healed of arthritis, of a terminal brain tumor, of terrifying psychological problems. I've met a teacher, a merchant, a politician who have given up their livelihoods to do God's work and let Him pay the bills. I've seen the prime downtown property called Las Alas, and I've heard a Presbyterian realtor explain how it came to be bought for a song by a Catholic priest in a deal only God could have closed.

For me, the time for skepticism has long passed. I believe that the power of God has been unleashed in the OLYC ministries in a way most people, even most believing Christians, could never have imagined. But believing that creates a whole new problem.

If God is really operating so powerfully through the OLYC ministries, you'd think the results would be bigger. After more than 35 years of it, El Paso and Juarez should be almost a new Garden of Eden. Or the front porch of heaven. Or at least a place where you can *tell* God has been at work—more faith, less sin, less disease, more sharing of food and possessions, than in your home town or mine. Or maybe not that—maybe instead a gigantic spiritual battlefield where the work of God and the work of Satan would be so obvious that the village atheist would have to acknowledge it and the biggest slacker would have to take sides.

Well, nothing like that has happened. Cross the street from Las Alas or drive half a mile past the food bank, and Juarez is just as poor, El Paso just as indifferent, and the whole area just as sinful and heathen as 35

155

years ago. I don't know what percentage of El Paso and Juarez residents have even heard of OLYC or its work, but I can tell you there are plenty who haven't. As it has for more than three decades, the community, or rather the Spirit, continues to do very big things on a very small scale. And I don't understand. With power so great, why is everything still so small?

This was not a question I was looking forward to asking Father Thomas. He was a lot of fun to talk to, with his tightly-wound Jesuit intellect and his totally unwound sense of humor, but he wasn't an easy interview. He refused to be glib, and if he didn't agree with the way a question was framed, he didn't hesitate to say so. So I was more than a little nervous about asking a question that seemed to throw doubt on everything he was doing.

But he didn't have any problem at all with the way *this* question was framed. He'd been thinking about it himself, for years. And he had an answer—the last answer I would have expected. Like the wealthy ruler who asked Jesus about eternal life (Luke 18:18-25), OLYC still has one thing lacking: single-minded, self-emptying commitment. In concrete language, there aren't enough people like Norma Garcia Reuter, or Sergio and Lucia Conde, or Delia Ramos, or the gang at the ranch. Plenty of people are willing to give a good effort, but not many are willing to give *themselves*, without reservation.

"People are only ready to go a certain distance with the Lord," Father Thomas said. "They're not ready to go all the way. Sin comes in, and that's as far as they're willing to go with the Lord."

Sin? At OLYC? Not that you and I would notice. Most of the people who hang around the ministries have their sex lives pretty well in order. Not many are into drug and alcohol abuse. Not many are living like the rich and famous, or even trying to. Not many are spending their energy on getting to be rock stars or professional athletes or governor of Texas. But it's all a question of priorities, Father Thomas said. Too many people are busy living their own lives even as they try to serve God, pursuing their own plans and above all worrying about making a living. And yes, he said, that's sin.

"There's obvious sin," Father Thomas said, "and then there's lack of trust in God. God wants to bring us to Himself, but a lot of times we don't want to go to God, and that's what sin is. The major sin is not loving God with your whole heart and soul.

"In my experience people are trapped in what they do. You say 'let's go to Juarez Monday and evangelize,' and they can't come. They have to work or go to school or on vacation or whatever. The challenge is too great, and they back off." It isn't that all Christians are necessarily called to quit their jobs, Father Thomas said. In fact, some people are called to make a ministry of the jobs they already have, like Tommy and Ceci Barrientos; and anyway, a major step like quitting work requires a lot of discernment (see also Chapter 12). But lack of commitment also shows up in the face of challenges a lot smaller than quitting a job; too many people won't even

157

change short-term plans or put up with temporary discomfort.

"They say 'I won't go such-and-such a place. It isn't air conditioned,'" Father Thomas said. "And it's pretty hard to get anyone to work in ministry on Super Bowl Sunday. They'll never get around to the big things because they can't do the little things."

But if the little things are inconvenient, the big things are terrifying. The big thing everybody needs to do to make ministries like those at OLYC really catch fire is to obey Jesus' demand from Luke 14:33: renounce all possessions, and that includes not only our money and our goods but our time and even our loved ones. We may or may not actually be asked to live without them, but we are asked to stop hanging on to them.

"The disposal of our possessions is a practical matter that's up to God," Father Thomas said. "Renouncing them is a spiritual exercise that everybody has to do to be a disciple. It's very painful. People will do it and take it back a few hours later.

"The key point is that what people say is 'mine' is not theirs. Everything belongs to God, and it should be used as He wants and not as if I owned it. I'm just an administrator."

The whole OLYC operation is based on believing literally and concretely in things most people, even most good Christians, don't believe in the same literal way. "Most of the churches are saying you've got to be practical," says Jim Gallagher. "God says 'don't worry,' and the first thing we do, we close the door of the car

158

and start worrying. But Father Thomas is saying God's Word is not always practical."

Unfortunately, when it comes to the idea that it's possible to renounce all our possessions without ending up in the gutter, it isn't only *other* Christians who don't believe it. It's a tough sell at OLYC too.

"The Bible says seek first the kingdom of God, and all these things will be added to you" (Luke 12:31, paraphrased), Father Thomas said. "We do not believe that. It's not preached, it's not believed, it's not acted on. As a large group, we [at OLYC] don't believe it. I believe it, and the people who live at the ranch believe it, but most of the people at the prayer meeting don't believe it."

What would happen if everybody *did* believe it, and not only believed it but lived by it? Father Thomas had a story to tell about that. It involves four tiny squashes, "as big as my fingers," the very first food grown at the Lord's Ranch back in 1975.

Those, the community decided, were the Lord's squashes, so they were given to a poor elderly woman the group knew. And as the harvest increased, to maybe a pound a week, the volunteers kept giving it away. "None of us ever tasted that squash," Father Thomas said.

Then, after about eight weeks, volunteers went out to pick the usual pound and tossed it into a full-size garbage bag. They left the bag lying on the ground for a few minutes, and when they went back to get it, it was so full of squash they couldn't carry it.[5]

Surprise? Not to Father Thomas. "Jesus says 'give, and it will be given to you.'" (Luke 6:38).

And that, Father Thomas said, is the answer to the question I was asking earlier. It's going to take that kind of willingness to believe in God's promises and give everything to Him before El Paso and Juarez burst into the flames of the Holy Spirit. But there is a lot more at stake than Juarez and El Paso.

At the beginning of Matthew 10, Jesus sends the 12 disciples out on their first mission. He tells them to proclaim that "The kingdom of Heaven has come near." (verse 7). And in the very next verse, He tells them "You received without payment; give without payment." That, Father Thomas said, is no coincidence. "Giving without payment" is the key to the coming of the kingdom, then and now.

"As soon as we start to take that seriously, we're going to see the conversion of the world," he said. "But most Christians don't believe the kingdom of God is near, and they don't like the changes they have to make to experience the kingdom of God.

---

[5] Mary Ann Halloran testifies to similar multiplications of produce, on the same basis, after she arrived at The Lord's Ranch the following year.

"The reign of God is near, but we have to change if we're going to experience it. The reign of God is held off if we won't change, for the rest of the world too."

# PART III: PUTTING IT TOGETHER

## CHAPTER 12: TRYING THIS AT HOME

Nobody lives in garbage dumps in my town. We do have a homeless population, but the poorest people who've found housing live in palaces compared to the folks in the Juarez shantytowns. Our welfare system is a long way from perfect, but it helps a lot: in theory, at least, just about everybody gets a basic level of food, clothing and medical care. It used to make me wonder whether there would be any place for an outfit like OLYC where I live.

Well, the answer is yes. There's a place for an outfit like OLYC in my town, and in your town, and everybody else's town. Because the point of the OLYC ministries isn't serving Christmas dinners at garbage dumps. It's obeying God. And Christians are called to obey God in every town.

Besides, there's always plenty to do, no matter where you live. For one thing, the Gospel always needs to be preached. For another, material poverty still destroys lives in my town and yours, even if not at the level it does in Juarez. And finally, not all poverty is material.

There's spiritual poverty, too: family breakdown, social conflict, personal aimlessness, sin of all kinds.

"There's tremendous spiritual poverty in the United States and Canada," Father Thomas said. "It's all over the place. It's not as stark and visible as material poverty, but it's just as important, and it needs to be dealt with."

So here is what was promised at the beginning of this book: a guide to following OLYC's example in your own home town. First comes a list of things to do to find out what direction you should take; then comes a list of things you need to watch out for if you want to have any chance of getting where you want to go.

---

## WHAT TO DO

**1. Search the Scriptures.** "Study the Scriptures very carefully, as a book to be obeyed rather than dissected," said Fr. Thomas. "Under the guidance of the Holy Spirit, find Scripture pertinent to your current situation."

This doesn't mean you don't need understanding, or an awareness of a Bible passage's context, or even the insights of critical scholarship sometimes. Amateur Bible-thumping can do a fair bit of harm; for example, Father Thomas said, "there's a lot of baloney out there about the Book of Revelation." One cure for this is following Church guidance. As far outside the Catholic mainstream as OLYC might look, the community never interprets the Bible in a way contrary to the teachings of the Church. Catholics trying this at home should follow the same rule; Christians in other churches should pay attention to responsible, Bible-honoring interpretations from the best scholarship available.

But at the same time, this should never be an excuse to hide in a comfortable stock interpretation of the Bible, in any church, or to disregard its challenge to us. The whole idea is to let God's Word take us far beyond what most church leaders ever suggest. And as for scholarly insights, the question of whether the book of Jonah is historical or whether a Gospel passage is Jesus' exact spoken words should never make us forget that it all counts as "Bible" and it's all God's Word to us, to be put into practice. "The Bible is meant to change our life," Father Thomas said. "Don't bother to read the Scriptures if it's not going to change your life."

**2. Ask God for direction.** Some years ago I decided I needed Father Thomas's advice on a new responsibility I had taken on in my own local church. I flew across half a continent to El Paso, mainly so I could talk to him face to face. He offered several pieces of advice, but the main piece of advice he gave me was "don't ask me—ask God."

When you're done searching the Scriptures, "pray for God's guidance on what He wants you to do." Don't expect audible answers or anything like that; just be open. The more you pray, the more you'll be in touch with God and able to discern what He is telling you. And of course, the more power you'll have to carry out whatever He tells you.

**3. Look around.** What's happening in your town is part of God's message concerning His will for you.

"Observe the circumstances you find yourself in," Father Thomas said. "You're probably not going to start a soup kitchen in Beverly Hills."

What opportunities has God given you? What do you have the human resources to do? Where is the material poverty? Where is the spiritual poverty? What part of God's work has been left undone in your city? What people's needs has He pushed in front of you?

**4. Make your plans, but hang loose.** Once you've discerned the needs, you'll have to make plans, just like any football coach or corporate CEO. But now is not the time to stop listening to God. He'll still be talking to you—at this point, mainly by wrecking your plans like a blitzing linebacker.

"You've got to have human planning," Father Thomas said. "It just isn't going to work. Whatever we plan is not God's plan. So do your planning, but realize it's going to change. You need a plan so you'll have something to change."

## WHAT TO WATCH OUT FOR

**Commitment without discernment.** You have to be ready to go where God leads you, but trying to get ahead of Him causes nothing but trouble. If you quit your day job in the middle of Chapter 11, the odds are you made a mistake.

Discernment of personal vocation is too big a topic for this chapter, or even this whole book. But it's still necessary to give a warning. God speaks to us in many ways, and it's important to listen to all of them. For example, if you have family responsibilities, that's one of God's comments on your plan to quit your job. You should be *willing* to quit, for sure, but you'll need a lot more evidence, discerned over time and with the help of trustworthy spiritual advisers and fellow-Christians, before you know God actually wants you to *do* it. The same goes for other major projects: follow God as He leads, one step at a time. He'll take you a long way before you know it.

"The devil deceives good people by getting them to do good things God does not want them to do," Father Thomas said. "He can't get them to sin grossly, so he gets them to do things that appear to be good that aren't God's will. You need to discern whether God is asking you to do *this* good thing, now, in this way."

**Personal sin.** While you're busy trying to follow God's specific will for you, you'd better be sure you're following His general will for everybody. Keep the commandments, including the ones you don't like or haven't been keeping up until now.

Staying away from sin yourself is a simple matter (not easy, maybe, but simple). What's more complicated is knowing what to do about sin in other members of the group you work with. You can't monitor everybody's life in detail, and you can't limit the group to canonized saints. "You've got to give everybody a chance to serve God," Father Thomas said, "and they don't all start out at top speed."

On the other hand, sin can't be allowed to wreck a ministry. Nobody should be in a position where his or her sin creates a specific danger. For example, anyone with past occult involvement which hasn't been cleansed should be kept out of leadership. A man whose sex life is not in order shouldn't be counseling women.

Beyond that, there are no blanket rules. A person's sin has to be evaluated on how it affects the whole group. The human body can stand a certain concentration of germs, but above that level it will get sick. In just the same way, the Christian body can absorb only so much sin on the part of its members and still be effective. Sometimes common sense will give the answer: a quarrelsome member may be tolerable in a group of 40 but not a group of 10. Sometimes it's necessary to look at the fruit of the ministry: if the sin lessens the fruit, it's too much.

In any case, there should be good moral teaching and calls to repentance within the group, and if there are any special problems, that teaching may need to be stepped up. "When you turn up the heat, [problem] people tend to leave," Father Thomas said.

**Corporate sin.** This is sin built into the ministry itself, and it's a bigger problem than personal sin. "Corporate sin is a bigger problem because it *is* corporate," Father Thomas said, and not only in Christian ministries. Exploiting workers as a group, for example, is worse than stealing from individuals.

The community must be strictly honest in all its work. No lying, no stealing, no misrepresentation, no leaving debts unpaid, no breaking promises, no dishonest fundraising. "God will not build on what is not upright and just," Father Thomas said, pointing to Isa. 28:16-17. "He may use it for a while, but then He'll sweep it away."

**Disunity.** Unity in the ministry is essential. Participants should love one another and be of one mind and heart, at least as far as the work of the ministry is concerned. "An individual alone, no matter how qualified, cannot be as effective as the body of Christ working together," Father Thomas said. "That's why we're able to do so much [at OLYC]."

**Opposition.** Don't expect any of this to be easy. The body of Christ has enemies in low places. "Satan is the god of this world," Father Thomas said. "You're always dealing with that, whether you recognize it or not." Satan can manipulate everything in the world to some degree, even the Church. Along with triumphs like the Christmas dinner multiplication and the purchase of Las Alas, OLYC has a long history of attacks, from mysterious tire blowouts to frivolous lawsuits. Human opposition is a problem, too, not only outside the Church but within it: touchy issues from racism to abortion have been played down in the pulpit over the years for fear of offending the flock, Father Thomas said.

But none of this is any reason to be afraid. It just goes with the territory, and Christians need to rely on a Lord who is stronger than the enemy.

"If you ask an individual to get out of the kingdom of Satan in any way he's involved in it, there's going to be

169

a struggle," Father Thomas said. "The forces of Satan are going to struggle, and the individual himself is going to struggle, and that brings about persecution.

"When the Gospel is preached in any vigorous way, it generates persecution. In our country the Church is generally chicken. We're afraid of persecution and we're often ashamed of Jesus and His message."

If persecution can be avoided by foresight and wisdom, without betraying the Gospel or dodging our duty, that's fine; "there's no sense in looking for persecution," Father Thomas said.

But when persecution isn't avoidable, he said, Christians can take comfort from Rom. 8:28: "We know that in everything God works for good with those who love him, who are called according to his purpose."

"Just keep going straight ahead," Father Thomas said. "Don't worry about it. God gives strength to withstand persecution, and He turns it into something good."

# EPILOGUE

Father Rick Thomas died at the Lord's Ranch in the early evening of May 8, 2006. He was 78. He had had a skin melanoma removed by surgery in 2000, and metastasis of that cancer, followed by cardio-pulmonary failure, was given as the cause of death.

He had been sick since the August before his death, with stomach complaints and other symptoms. His weight dropped to 95 pounds on a six-foot frame. "He used to joke about the variety of symptoms he had," says Ellen Hogarty.

Jokes or not, he also came to believe that his illness had a spiritual origin, and that it was his job to unite his sufferings with the sufferings of Jesus. As his body got weaker, his prayer grew more intense. "I want you to know," Hogarty told eight hundred people who jammed Las Alas for visitation and the rosary the day before his funeral, "that he prayed for everyone who is here tonight. He had a lot of time to pray."

He nearly died in December. The ministries carried on without him, not limping along but growing, financially and in every other way. "That's very consoling to me," he said shortly before his death. "As crippled up as I am, things are going along fine." Then he began to bounce back, and on Jan. 29 celebrated his first Mass in seven weeks—seated, but in a booming voice. He resumed meeting weekly with the Young Shepherds. He believed he would eventually be back to full strength physically; mentally he was at full strength right to the end, sense of humor and all, and his preaching didn't weaken any either, even when his recovery stalled and his voice sank almost to a whisper in early April.

The Sunday after Easter, Divine Mercy Sunday, he celebrated a two-hour Mass including an hour of teaching, focused especially on the reading from Acts 4:32-37, the passage that says nobody was needy in the early Church because nobody claimed personal ownership of anything.

"We don't do that," he told a capacity crowd. "The Church doesn't do it. We're disobedient. We need God's mercy... That's why there's needy people in Juarez. There was no needy person among them, but we have thousands and thousands of needy people among us. We can give ourselves all kinds of excuses, but it comes down to 'we are disobedient.'"

It was his last sermon. Not long after, he relapsed. For the last week of his life, he was bedridden. The end came at 6:25 p.m. of one of his better days. He was in good spirits and ate more than usual. But he was short of breath in the afternoon. Hogarty and Michael Reuter were with him and when he called for "Scripture!" Hogarty began executing Psalm 23. "No," he responded. "Isaiah 35!"

As Hogarty began reading ("Here is your God... He will come and save you.") (verse 4), he began staring off to one side. "I said, 'who are you seeing? Is somebody coming for you?'" He smiled, and laughed his characteristic soundless laugh. Hogarty started CPR and he laughed again. "As fast as that, he was gone."

The day of the rosary, the body lay all day at Las Alas in the plywood coffin, made by Reuter. Hundreds of people came in to say goodbye, touch the body, and pray. Eight hundred turned out for the rosary itself. Afterward, the building shook with praise music, and the conga line snaked by within two feet of the coffin; some people even gave it cheerful taps of greeting as they skipped by. Then it was testimony time. One woman had had a grapefruit-sized tumor disappear after Father Thomas prayed over her. Another told of how her marriage had been healed after Father prayed and also intervened with her husband. Yet another had a friend who received a potentially life-saving message from Father Thomas in a dream after his death.

Joe Yañez of Dallas talked about how he had first come to the prayer meetings as a pot-addicted teenager, always leaving early. He had been to only three meetings when he skipped one, then returned the following week to be told that Father Thomas had missed him. Father Thomas took him to the Lord's Ranch to work, and today he is a successful drug counselor with a 25-year marriage.

Bob Statton, a Baptist from Midland, Texas, who has gotten members of his own denomination involved in OLYC ministries on the Juarez side of the river, summed it up: "He is dancing with the Lord now," he told the crowd. "There's nothing better than that."

The next day, more than 1,000 squeezed into Sacred Heart, the Jesuit parish a few blocks from Las Alas, for the funeral Mass. The business suits of leading citizens mingled with the simple but neat clothing of the poor and the religious T-shirts of a youth group visiting the ranch. Bishop Armando Ochoa of El Paso was chief celebrant. The community chose some of Father Thomas's favorite passages for Scripture readings, each printed in the program in one language and read aloud in the other: Deut. 6:4-9, about loving God with all our hearts; Psalm 68, scattering God's enemies; Phil. 4:4-9, keeping our minds on edifying things; and Matt. 25: 31-46, our duty to the least among us.

As Reuter read from Philippians, Father Thomas's voice almost seemed to join with St. Paul's in a message for the whole congregation: "Keep on doing what you have learned and received and heard and seen in me," (Phil 4:9a). But Bishop Ramirez, whose Las Cruces diocese includes the Lord's Ranch, had the last word about an unconventional, sometimes controversial, ultra-demanding priest.

Father Thomas, he said in Spanish, was not some hippie out on the margins of society. "He was at the center, in the heart of the Church—in the heart of Jesus."

In a final act of obedience to his order, Father Thomas, who had wanted to be buried at the Lord's Ranch, was in fact buried with other prominent El Paso Jesuits (and the gunslinger John Wesley Hardin) in the city's dusty Concordia Cemetery, next to a busy freeway. Hundreds of people stood sweating in mid-90s sun for the very last chance to say goodbye, and all who wished were allowed to help fill the grave with shovels of earth.

Afterward, most returned to Las Alas for a potluck lunch. The food wasn't multiplied, so far as I know, but it didn't run out.

# AFTERWORD

## THE KINGDOM OF GOD HAS COME NEAR

The words at the head of this chapter are from Jesus' first recorded sermon, His first words in what most Bible scholars believe was the first of the Gospels to be written (Mark 1:15). Bible scholars of all types agree that the kingdom (or "reign") of God is one of the most important themes of Jesus' preaching. Unfortunately, scholars don't agree about what He meant by that, but it's pretty clear His first disciples concluded after the Resurrection that the kingdom had arrived, or at least begun arriving. (It won't be established in all its fullness until Jesus comes back.) It's also pretty clear that they thought of the kingdom as something people would notice, and as based on the power of God, not just on a more enlightened human approach to life.

Almost certainly, the early Christians expected Jesus to come back and complete the kingdom in their own lifetimes. That didn't happen, of course, but still the Church carried on, and Christians continue to carry on almost 20 centuries later. What we're carrying on with,

177

whether we think of it that way or not, is a belief that God *has* intervened in power through Jesus, and that the kingdom of God *has* at least begun to arrive. I'd go so far as to say that all truly effective Christians through the centuries have believed that the kingdom is real enough to live in, and have in fact chosen to live in it. That's what makes them effective.

What does all this have to do with OLYC? Father Thomas and his friends have chosen to live in the kingdom of God more completely than anyone I have ever met. In living their lives by trust in the Bible's promises, they have brought the kingdom of God more fully to earth. And sure enough, it *is* based on God's power, and people *do* notice it. And most importantly, for me as an individual, they have showed what the kingdom is like, point by point, in a way I have been looking for all my life.

**God is real.** I knew for a long time, as I clung by my fingernails to a rather vague Christian faith, that an abstract, philosophical God just wouldn't do. The village atheist who doesn't believe in God because he can't see Him has a point; the same point is made in a much more sophisticated way by a group of modern philosophers called logical positivists, who say that concepts like "God" are meaningless if they can't be tested by the difference they make in the everyday world. And the differences Christians often point to, like better moral behavior (if that actually happens) or the emotional support people get from their religion, aren't enough to meet that kind of test. They can always be written off as purely human matters that have nothing to do with any external reality.

At OLYC, on the other hand, God makes a much more concrete sort of difference. People get healed. Obstacles get overcome. Food gets multiplied. People's hearts change 180 degrees in a matter of minutes. Fancy real estate falls into the lap of a group with nowhere near enough money to buy it. God pays the bills. These are all just the sort of things a real God, the king who reigns in His kingdom, would do. Of course, these claims all sound pretty far-fetched, and a lot of people will refuse to believe them, or will find some other way to explain them. But the OLYC people have been taking them at face value for more than 35 years, and it works so well that it's the denials and the alternative explanations that end up sounding far-fetched. Here, at last, is a God worth believing in, both intellectually and practically.

**God is king.** If God is the Creator, He gave us everything we have. If He is real, He is the best possible thing to rely on. And if He is king, He is our sovereign and entitled to perfect obedience. So it only makes sense to be totally committed to Him—in personal morality, in life priorities, in meeting needs and dealing with problems. Even I can *see* that, but the people at OLYC are more consistent than I am. They're *living* as subjects of the King.

**God's reign covers everything.** Real kingdoms, even in this world, are well-rounded operations. A lot goes on in them besides ceremonies at the royal court. People grow food and eat dinner, get married and raise children, play sports and study at universities. And all of it is subject to the king, one way or another.

The OLYC community approaches the kingdom of God on just that basis: it includes everything. This shows up in several different ways.

First of all, the ministries cover, maybe not literally everything, but the full range of human activities. There's worship of God. There's preaching the Gospel. There's feeding the hungry, and providing medical care, and sometimes even housing or clean water when the need comes up. There's earthly political activity, and what might be called heavenly political activity (spiritual warfare). Everything is important, because everything belongs to God. OLYC and its work also reach out to every*body*, Anglo as well as Hispanic, healthy as well as sick, young as well as old, unbelievers as well as believers, criminals as well as the law-abiding, rich and middle-class as well as poor, visitors as well as locals. God is everybody's king.

Secondly, the thinking at OLYC takes everything into account, convenient or not. When I hear about people as far out on a limb of faith as this group is, I expect them to be simplistic. It's human nature to simplify, and the easiest way (for example) to take the Bible as literally as the OLYC community does would be to ignore or deny the difficulties presented by modern science and critical Bible scholarship. At OLYC that doesn't happen. Father Thomas, in particular, knew all about the difficulties, and took them seriously; but the promise of God and its fulfillment in the group's experience over the years tip the scales, and the group relies totally on the Bible despite the difficulties. It's the same way with everything else: the community follows an extremely conservative Christian moral code without ignoring or despising human weakness; it trusts in God to pay the bills and remove the obstacles, without ever giving up common sense or practical planning; it decides on simple policies and projects after full consideration of all the complexities involved. I don't know how many members of the community care about this, but it's important to me: the childlike obedience and trust in God at OLYC are carried out with no loss of intellectual honesty and responsibility.

Finally, just as life in an earthly kingdom includes activities of all sorts, so does life in the kingdom of God for the people at OLYC. Nothing could be further from one-dimensional. Their focus on worshipping God and serving the poor doesn't deprive them of the enjoyments of the world God created. They live simply, but they relish their food and their leisure and one another's company; the fact that they talk about Jesus more than any other topic doesn't keep them from also talking about football or local politics, or even making outrageous puns. They swim and play board games and read novels and go on vacation, and they are never in a hurry. Life is still "normal," or better than normal.

**God's kingdom is joyous.** If God is perfect goodness, His kingdom should be a happy place. And at OLYC, it is. It shows in worship: no three-hour prayer meeting has ever been shorter than the one at Las Alas on Wednesday nights. It shows in human affection, between community members and also toward visitors, even people who only stay a few days. It shows in the enthusiasm on the ministries and the relaxing pace of life at the Lord's Ranch. The subjects of God's kingdom at OLYC are simply the happiest people I have ever met.

I still don't live in the kingdom of God, not by OLYC standards anyway. There's a huge gap between knowing the principles for "trying this at home" in chapter 12 and being in the spiritual shape to do it. In my terms, it takes three things to be an OLYC Christian: first, believing in Jesus, the Bible, and (for Catholics) certain Catholic teachings in a lot more concrete terms than most people you meet in church do; second, praying so much it takes over your whole day; and third, throwing your personal comfort zone out with the rest of the trash.

After 20 years of knowing the OLYC crowd, I'm totally on side with that first point, but I haven't really gotten the hang of the other two. Like most sincere Christians, I pray and give money to the poor and spend time working for my local church; but I fit the work of the kingdom into the rest of my life, rather than the other way around, and my motto isn't so much "what would Jesus do?" as "what will Jesus let me get away with?" That changes a little, for the moment, on visits to El Paso, when I help deliver food in Juarez, or go into the jail, or pray in the chapel at the Lord's Ranch; but it all goes back to "normal" when I get home.

No, I'm wrong. It doesn't *all* go back to normal. One thing has changed forever. Now that I've seen the OLYC community, I can never again rationalize my failures to live in the kingdom as anything other than laziness, cowardice and bad priorities. Because the kingdom of God covers not only every*thing* and every*body* but every*where*. I don't have to go to El Paso to live in the kingdom. My own city will do fine, and so will yours. Wherever we live, the kingdom of God has come near. We need only reach out and take hold of it. It's real, and it's there to be lived in.

May God grant us the faith and courage to do it.

ADDITIONAL COPIES OF THIS BOOK MAY BE OBTAINED
BY CONTACTING:

**OUR LADY'S YOUTH CENTER**
**P.O. BOX 1371**
**EL PASO, TX 79948-1371**
**915-533-9122**

**EMAIL***:* olyc77@gmail.com


**FOR MORE INFORMATION GO TO:**

www.fatherrickthomas.com

www.thelordsranchvado.com

www.lasalascommunity.com